DIE ESSENZ DER DINGE
DESIGN UND DIE KUNST DER REDUKTION

THE ESSENCE OF THINGS
DESIGN AND THE ART OF REDUCTION

Vitra Design Museum

KATALOG / CATALOGUE

Herausgeber / Editors:
Mathias Schwartz-Clauss, Alexander von Vegesack

Lektorat / Copy editors:
Kirsten Thietz, Ariel Krill

Übersetzungen / Translations:
Julia Taylor Thorson

Bildrecherche / Picture research:
Martin Hartung, Melanie Dietz, Kathleen Schwabe

Grafik, Satz / Graphic design, typesetting:
Thorsten Romanus

Produktionsleitung / Production:
Jörn Strüker

Vertrieb / Distribution:
Hanna Benndorf, Irma Hager

Lithographie, Druck / Lithography, printing:
GZD, Ditzingen

© Vitra Design Museum und Autoren /
and authors, 2010

AUTOREN / AUTHORS

DIRK BAECKER ist Soziologe und lehrt Kulturtheorie
und Kulturanalyse an der Zeppelin Universität
in Friedrichshafen am Bodensee.

Dirk Baecker is a sociologist and teaches cultural
theory and analysis at Zeppelin University in
Friedrichshafen, Germany.

MARTIN HARTUNG arbeitet international als
freier Kunsthistoriker und Publizist.

Martin Hartung works internationally as a
freelance art historian and journalist.

WIEBKE LANG ist freie Journalistin, Ausstellungs-
kuratorin und Designerin.

Wiebke Lang is a freelance journalist, exhibition
curator, and designer.

MATHIAS SCHWARTZ-CLAUSS ist Kunsthistoriker
und als Kurator am Vitra Design Museum tätig.

Mathias Schwartz-Clauss is an art historian and
a curator at Vitra Design Museum.

ISBN 978-3-931936-50-1

AUSSTELLUNG / EXHIBITION

Kurator / Curator:
Mathias Schwartz-Clauss

Assistenzkurator / Assistant Curator:
Martin Hartung

Berater / Advisors:
Rolf Fehlbaum, Naoto Fukasawa,
Ayako Kamozawa, Stefan Karp, Mateo Kries,
Jasper Morrison

Objektrecherche / Object research:
Serge Mauduit

Objektbearbeitung / Object handling:
Grazyna Ubik

Objektlogistik / Object logistics:
Boguslaw Ubik-Perski

Ausstellungsgestaltung / Exhibition design:
Dieter Thiel

Technische Leitung / Technical directors:
Stefanie Fricker, Thomas Schmidhauser

Installationsbau / Installations:
Michael Simolka

Medientechnik / Media technology:
Gregor Bielser

Ausstellungsgrafik / Exhibition graphics:
Thorsten Romanus

Ausstellungstournee / Exhibition tour:
Reiner Packeiser, Isabel Serbeto

Begleitprogramm / Supporting activities:
Kilian Jost

Führungen / Guided tours:
Anneliese Gastel

Produkte / Products:
Marine Gallian

GESAMTPROJEKT / OVERALL PROJECT

Operative Leitung / Operative management:
Marc Zehntner

Presse- und Öffentlichkeitsarbeit /
Press and publicity: Isabelle Beilfuss, Gianoli PR

WIR DANKEN SEHR HERZLICH /
WE EXTEND OUR SINCERE THANKS TO

Shigeru Ban,
Rainer Baum,
Jean Boghossian,
Roberto Boghossian,
Georg Böhringer,
Franco Clivio,
Hanns-Peter Cohn,
Luc Delay,
Maria Cristina Didero,
Jochen Eisenbrand,
Madeleine Hoffmann,
James Irvine,
Sebastian Jacobi,
Reiner Judd,
Carde Meyer,
Robert Nachbargauer,
Andreas Nutz,
Optik Burkhart GmbH,
Thomas Rempen,
Bernhard Schweyer,
Sparkasse Markgraeflerland,
Hubert Steins,
Friedolin Strüker,
Ratan Tata,
Heinz Witthoeft,
Rüdiger Wulf,
Johann Zacher und Familie / and family,
und der Arbeitsgemeinschaft des Vitra Design Museums
/ and the entire team at Vitra Design Museum.

Unterstützt durch /   Worldwide Sponsor
Supported by
Vitra GmbH

INHALT / CONTENTS

VORWORT

Man mag darüber streiten, was früher da war: das Bedürfnis des Menschen, Dinge zu dekorieren, oder sein Bestreben, sie einfacher und reduzierter zu gestalten. Für das Design aber lässt sich eindeutig feststellen, welches dieser beiden Prinzipien dominiert: die Kunst der Reduktion. Seitdem sich Design im Verlauf des 19. Jahrhunderts als eigenständige Disziplin etabliert hat, ist das Bemühen um eine Vereinfachung der Form, der Herstellung und der Benutzung von Objekten eine der wichtigsten Triebkräfte für die Designentwicklung. In dieser Suche verbindet sich das Ideal einer rationalen industriellen Produktion mit dem Traum des Menschen von einem einfacheren Leben.

Obwohl Reduktion also eine Konstante der Designgeschichte ist, sind ihre Ergebnisse so vielfältig wie ihre unterschiedlichen Stile und Aufgabenstellungen. So wurde die Reduktion eines Objekts in bestimmten Epochen aus industriellen Herstellungsverfahren entwickelt, während in anderen eher die Materialausnutzung oder die Zeichenhaftigkeit des Endprodukts im Vordergrund standen. Für die jeweilige Ästhetik wurden zuweilen außereuropäische Vorbilder herangezogen, in anderen Fällen wiederum einfache bäuerliche Möbel oder Anregungen aus der Minimal Art. Dass Reduktion auch keinen Widerspruch mehr zu der wachsenden technischen Komplexität unserer Umgebung bilden muss, haben in den letzten Jahren Produkte wie der iPod bewiesen. Im Verlauf des 20. Jahrhunderts hat sich darüber hinaus gezeigt, dass die Suche nach Reduktion im Design nicht entlang der üblichen kunstideologischen Fronten verläuft. Hat nicht selbst die so genannte Postmoderne wunderbare Beispiele reduzierter Gestaltung hervorgebracht, obwohl sie ursprünglich gegen eine allzu rigide Reduktionsideologie der Moderne angetreten ist?

Mit den ökonomischen Entwicklungen der jüngsten Zeit ist schließlich auch die Frage wieder aktuell geworden, ob ein reduziertes Design gerade in Krisensituationen besondere Konjunktur hat und ob es gar zu deren Bewältigung beitragen kann. Natürlich schwingt auch diese Frage in der Ausstellung „Die Essenz der Dinge – Design und die Kunst der Reduktion" mit, doch sie ist nicht der Fokus des Projekts. Die Ausstellung und das vorliegende Buch zeigen vielmehr die enorme Vielfalt von Gründen, die die Suche nach reduziertem Design haben kann – und eine ebenso große Vielzahl an Ergebnissen. Dabei wird deutlich: Je komplexer unsere Umwelt wird, desto wichtiger wird es, in ihrer Gestaltung Einfachheit, Funktionalität, Reduktion und Überschaubarkeit anzustreben. Auch wenn dieses Unterfangen immer komplizierter wird.

Alexander von Vegesack

PREFACE

One can argue incessantly about what came first: the human need to decorate things or the striving for simpler and reduced forms. In the case of design, however, it is quite clear which principle dominates: the art of reduction. Ever since design asserted itself as an independent discipline over the course of the nineteenth century, the endeavour to simplify the form, fabrication, and use of objects has been a key force in its development. In this quest, the ideal of rational industrial production joins together with the dream of a simpler way of life.

Although reduction is hence a constant of design history, its outcomes are as multifaceted as its various styles and functions. In certain epochs the reduction of objects stemmed from industrial manufacturing processes, while other eras gave greater weight to the utilization of material and to the symbolic character of the end product. Certain aesthetics have drawn on non-European sources, while others took inspiration from simple peasant furniture or Minimal Art. The fact that reduction is no longer inconsistent with the growing technical complexity of our environment has been demonstrated in recent years by products like the iPod. Moreover, developments in the twentieth century have shown that pursuit of reduction in design does not always proceed along the usual fronts of artistic ideologies. Even so-called postmodernism spawned some marvellous examples of reduced design, despite its initial stance as an opposition to an all too rigid creed of modernist reduction.

Finally, recent economic developments have brought resurgent interest to the question of whether reduced design is particularly in demand during periods of crisis and whether it can even contribute to overcoming the challenges that present themselves during such times. This question certainly features in the exhibition "The Essence of Things: Design and the Art of Reduction" yet does not constitute its main focus. Instead, the exhibition and the book at hand aim to show the tremendous diversity of motivations behind the aspiration towards reduced design—and the equally wide variety of its outcomes. One thing becomes clear. As our environment grows in complexity, its design requires ever-greater simplicity, functionality, reduction, and comprehensibility. Even if the undertaking itself only becomes more and more complicated.

IN KÜRZE

Die großen und auffälligen Werke der Ingenieure, Architekten und Designer haben unsere Eltern und uns jahrzehntelang fasziniert. Das Projekt der Moderne, der Glaube an Werte wie „schneller, höher, weiter" und das begleitende visuelle und mediale Getöse haben dabei eine Haltung in den Hintergrund gedrängt, die in den 1960er Jahren von Dieter Rams („Mr. Braun") mit „weniger, aber besser" beschrieben wurde.

Heute ist diese Haltung wieder gefragt. Dank eines neuen, weltweiten Umweltbewusstseins und neuer wissenschaftlicher Erkenntnisse hat im vergangenen Jahrzehnt ein Umdenkungsprozess zu neuen Orientierungen geführt. Eine Produkt- und Industriekultur ist entstanden, die in allen Bereichen des Lebens zunehmend Erfolge feiert, weil „weniger" nicht als Verzicht wahrgenommen wird, sondern als Vorteil – und als Verpflichtung.

Eine kluge Ökobilanz, Nachhaltigkeit, Nützlichkeit, Gebrauchstüchtigkeit und die Ästhetik des Einfachen finden ein neues, angemessenes Interesse.

Als wir davon hörten, dass das Vitra Design Museum dieser Haltung und ihren Inspirationen eine Ausstellung mit dem Titel „Die Essenz der Dinge" widmen will, waren wir sofort bereit (und auch ein klein wenig stolz!), diese Ausstellung als Worldwide Sponsor zu unterstützen.

Für uns als Unternehmen ist ein solches Sponsoring Neuland – und wir haben wirklich nicht erwartet, wie interessant und inspirierend die Teilnahme an einem solchen Projekt in der Zusammenarbeit mit seinem Kurator und dem Museum sein kann.

So freut uns auch, dass während der Diskussionen, bei der Arbeit und über das Sponsoring hinaus noch ein weiteres Ausstellungsprojekt entstanden ist, mit dem wir in ein paar Monaten gemeinsam auf die unauffällig nützlichen, kleinen Dinge, die „Helden des Alltags", aufmerksam machen wollen.

Als erfolgreicher Hersteller von Produkten, die allein zur Kategorie der unbeachteten kleinen Genies gehören, weil sie „min=max" sind, wie wir sagen, wünschen wir der Ausstellung zur „Essenz der Dinge" überall auf der Welt die Beachtung, die sie verdient.

Steve Henn und Hans-Jürgen Meyer
Hi-Cone

IN SHORT

Big and bold works by engineers, architects, and designers have been a source of fascination for us and for our parents for decades. The project of modernism, the belief in values like "faster, higher, further", and the accompanying visual and media furore have ended up sidelining an approach described back in the 1960s by Dieter Rams ("Mr. Braun") as "less but better".

Today this approach is back in demand. Thanks to recent worldwide environmental awareness and new scientific discoveries, a process of rethinking has led over the past decade to fresh orientations and visions. With growing success, a culture of products and industry has taken root in all areas of life, with "less" no longer being perceived as a sacrifice—but as an advantage—and also as an obligation.

An intelligent ecological balance sheet, sustainability, utility, functionality, and the aesthetic of simplicity are met with new and well-deserved interest.

When we learned that Vitra Design Museum was planning to dedicate an exhibition entitled "The Essence of Things" to this approach and its sources of inspiration, we were instantly ready and willing (and even a little proud!) to support it as a worldwide sponsor.

For us as a company, sponsorship was uncharted territory —and we had no idea just how interesting and inspiring it could be to participate in such a project and work together with the curator and the museum.

Thus, we were again very pleased when the collaborative discussions and sponsorship activities led to plans for a further joint exhibition project. Set to open in a few months, this exhibition will aim to call attention to small, unobtrusively useful objects, the "heroes of the everyday".

As a successful manufacturer of products that uniformly fall into the category of unheeded little geniuses—true to the motto "min=max", as we like to say—we wish the exhibition on the "Essence of Things" all the international recognition it deserves.

PROLOG /
PROLOGUE

1

2

3

4

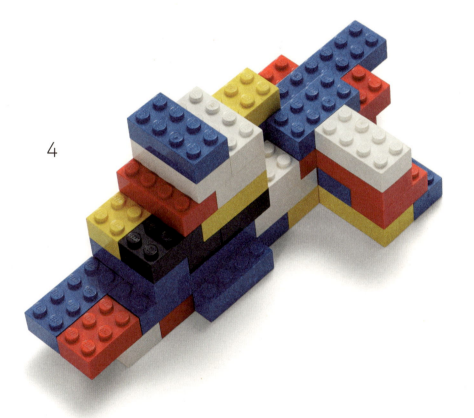

6

5

7

9

10

8

12

11

13

14

15

16

17

18

19

21

22

24

25

26

30

31

32

33

23

27

29

28

35

36

34

37

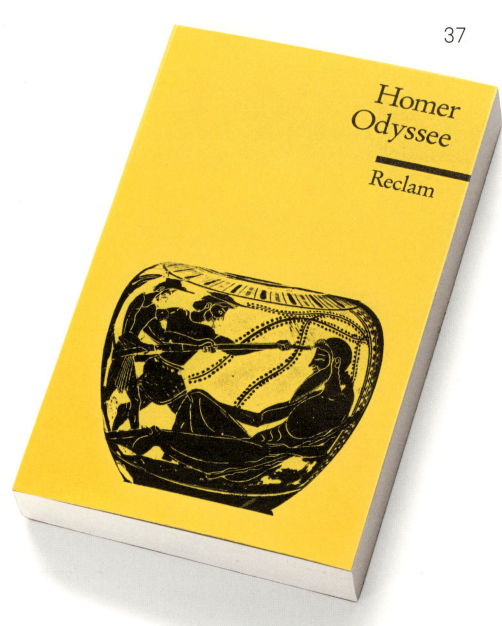

38

39

40

41

42

43

48

52

53

54

44

45

46

47

49

50

51

55

17

In den Beschreibungen der Werke erscheinen die Objektdaten, sofern bekannt, in der Reihenfolge / In the descriptions of the works, the object data (if known) is presented in the following order:

Autor (Erfinder, Herkunftsland) /
author (inventor, country of origin)

Art des Objekts /
type of object

Titel, Name(n) des Objekts /
title(s), name(s) of object

Datum des Entwurfs
(der Erfindung, der Markteinführung) /
date of design (invention, commercial launch)

Hersteller /
manufacturer

Maße /
dimensions

Materialien /
materials

Besitzer, Leihgeber /
owner, lender

PROLOG / PROLOGUE

1

Sushi-Imitationen / sushi imitations
undatiert / undated
IWASAKI Be-I, Tokyo
3 x 14 x 15,5 cm
Kunststoff / plastic
Collection Vitra Design Museum, Weil am Rhein

Sushi ist ein japanisches Gericht mit gesäuertem Reis und rohem Fisch, Gemüse, Ei oder Tofu, das in kleinen appetitlichen Häppchen gereicht wird. Traditionell werden die feinen Menüs mit einem hohen ästhetischen Anspruch zubereitet und in handlichen bento-Boxen serviert, die ein Streben nach Perfektion selbst in den einfachsten Dingen des Alltags repräsentieren, wie es für die japanische Kultur charakteristisch ist.

Presented in small, appetizing morsels, sushi is a Japanese dish consisting of vinegar-infused rice and raw fish, vegetables, egg, or tofu. Traditionally, the fine assortments are prepared to a high aesthetic standard and served in handy *bento* boxes, which represent the striving for perfection even in the simplest things of everyday life that characterizes so much of Japanese culture.

2

John Wesley Hyatt (Erfinder / inventor)
Billardkugel / billiard ball
1869 (Erfindung / invention)
Wagner Automaten, Buch
5,5 x 5,5 x 5,5 cm
Zelluloid /celluloid
Collection Vitra Design Museum, Weil am Rhein

3

NIVEA Cremedose / NIVEA cream tin
1911
Beiersdorf AG, Hamburg
4,4 x 11 x 11 cm
Aluminium / aluminium
Collection Mathias Schwartz-Clauss

Seit der Markteinführung dieses Hautpflegeproduktes unter der lateinischen Bezeichnung für „Schneeweiße" sorgt die schlichte, klare Gestaltung der blauen Dose als ein Archetyp konsequent umgesetzter Corporate Identity bis heute für die unmittelbare Identifizierung der Marke und des Herstellers.

Since the market launch of this skin care product under the Latin term for "snowy white", the simple and clear design of its blue canister has continued to provide instant identification of the brand and the manufacturer and serves as an archetype of consistently implemented corporate identity.

4

Ole Kirk Christiansen
Spielzeugbausteine / toy building blocks
LEGO-Steine / LEGO blocks
1958
LEGO, Billund
7 x 16,8 x 8 cm (in der abgebildeten Zusammenstellung / in the depicted constellation)
Acrylnitril-Butadien-Styrol-Copolymerisat (ABS)
Collection Gregor Bielser

Das von Ole Kirk Christiansen entwickelte modulare Baukastensystem für Kinder wurde 1932 zunächst aus Holz und ab 1949 aus Kunststoff hergestellt und in der heutigen Form erst 1958 patentiert. Der Name LEGO ist vom dänischen *leg godt* (deutsch: „spiel gut") abgeleitet. Mit den einfachen Grundbausteinen lassen sich im Mikrokosmos von LEGO Modelle aller möglichen Dinge bauen.

Developed by Ole Kirk Christiansen, this modular construction system for children was initially manufactured in wood from 1932 and later in plastic from 1949, with the current form not being patented until 1958. Its name is derived from the Danish *leg godt* ("play well"). Using the simple building blocks, models of every conceivable object and structure can be built in the microcosm of LEGO.

5

Harvey Ball (Erfinder / inventor)
Anstecker / button pin
Smiley
1963 (Erfindung / invention)
Zazzle.com, Inc., San José, CA
0,7 x 3,2 x 3,2 cm
Aluminium; Kunststoff / aluminium; plastic
Collection Vitra Design Museum, Weil am Rhein

Mit diesem Anstecker sollte ursprünglich nur das Betriebsklima in einer amerikanischen Versicherungsgesellschaft verbessert werden. Die unmittelbare Wirkung und der hohe Wiedererkennungswert des gelben kreisrunden Gesichts aus nur zwei Punkten und einem gebogenen Strich machten den *Smiley* aber schon bald weit über die Firma hinaus weltweit bekannt.

This button pin was originally conceived to improve the working environment at an American insurance company. Thanks to the instant impact and high recognition factor of the circular yellow face with just two round dots and a curving line, the *Smiley* soon spread beyond the company to achieve worldwide popularity.

6

William Taylor (Erfinder / inventor)
Golfball / golf ball
1905 (Erfindung / invention)
Dunlop Slazenger International Ltd., Shirebrook
4,3 x 4,3 x 4,3 cm
Kunststoff; Hartgummi / plastic; hard rubber
Collection Vitra Design Museum, Weil am Rhein

Sport und Militär sind Bereiche des Lebens, in denen sich Design ganz und gar auf die praktische Funktion konzentriert, da alles Übrige zur Gefahr werden kann oder zumindest den Erfolg beeinträchtigt. Um den Auftrieb der Bälle zu erhöhen, erfand 1905 der englische Mechaniker William Taylor die sogenannten *dimples*, hunderte von kleinen Dellen auf der Balloberfläche, durch die der Luftwiderstand verringert wird und der Ball bis zu viermal längere Distanzen überwinden kann.

Sports and the military are both fields in which design concentrates entirely on the practical function, since anything extraneous can lead to danger or at least to a negative impact on the chances of success. To maximize lift, in 1905 English engineer William Taylor came up with the idea of "dimples"—hundreds of small indentations on a golf ball's surface that minimize drag and allow the ball to travel up to four times as far.

7

Swatch Ltd. (2. von links / 2nd from left: Renzo Piano for Swatch Ltd.)
Armbanduhren / wrist watches
Genji / Jelly Piano / Dauntless / Jelly Fish / Big Tselim
1991 / 1999 / 2000 / 1986 / 1997
Swatch AG, Biel
0,9 x 22,9 x 3,5 cm (3. von links / 3rd from left:
0,5 x 22,9 x 3,5 cm)
verschiedene Materialien / mixed media
Collection Mathias Schwartz-Clauss und /
and Collection Studio 2

8

Dieter Rams
tragbarer Plattenspieler mit Radio / portable record player with radio
TP 1
1959
Braun oHG, Frankfurt/Main
5,4 x 23,5 x 16 cm
batteriebetriebener tragbarer Plattenspieler *P1* mit Radio *T4*, verschiedene Materialien / battery powered portable record player *P1* with radio *T4*, mixed media
Collection Vitra Design Museum, Weil am Rhein

Dieter Rams hat für Braun die Gestalt technischer Geräte von Grund auf neu definiert und sie wie bei militärisch genutzten Apparaten ganz auf eine einfache, effiziente und unmittelbar verständliche Bedienung ausgerichtet – ein Wegweiser für die gesamte Branche.

Dieter Rams redefined for Braun the shape of electrical appliances from the ground up and, as in equipment used by the military, oriented them towards simple, efficient, and intuitive handling and operation—a guidepost for the entire industry.

9

anonym / anonymous
Kleinstbildkamera / miniature camera
Minox EC
1981
Minox GmbH, Wetzlar
1,8 x 8 x 3 cm
Metall; Kunststoff; Glas / metal; plastic; glass
Collection Mathias Schwartz-Clauss

Diese klassische Kleinstbildkamera mit dem Filmformat 8 x 11 mm ist auch als Agenten- oder Spionagekamera bekannt. Das kleinste Serienmodell ist die *Minox EC* von 1981, mit deren Kunststoffgehäuse auch das Gewicht weiter reduziert wurde. Der Filmtransport und das Spannen des Verschlusses erfolgen schlicht durch Zusammendrücken und Auseinanderziehen des Gehäuses. Aus der vereinfachten Technik resultierte ein niedriger Kaufpreis.

This classic ultra-miniature camera, with an 8 x 11 millimetres film format, is also famous as a camera for spies and secret agents. The smallest mass-produced model is the *Minox EC* from 1981, whose plastic casing reduced the weight even further. The film advance and shutter are operated through a simple "push-and-pull" mechanism, which involves pushing the end of the camera housing in and out. The simplified technology also meant a low purchase price.

10

Jonathan Paul Ive
tragbares Medienabspielgerät / portable media player
iPod shuffle
2005
Apple Computer Inc., Cupertino, CA
2,73 x 4,12 x 1,05 cm
verschiedene Materialien / mixed media
Collection Vitra Design Museum, Weil am Rhein

11

Medikament / medicine
Globuli (Eupatorium Perfoliatum, C200)
undatiert / undated
Firma Remedia, Eisenstadt
0,1 x 0,1 x 0,1 cm (je Pille / per pill)
Collection Mathias Schwartz-Clauss

Globuli sind kleine Zuckerkügelchen, die in der homöopathischen Medizin Anwendung finden. Dadurch, dass die unterschiedlichen Wirkstoffe erst nach vielen Verdünnungsschritten, das so genannte Potenzieren, beigegeben werden, soll sich ihre Wirkung verstärken.

Globules are little balls of sugar used in homeopathic medicine. To strengthen the effect, the various active agents are only added after numerous dilution steps, otherwise referred to as potentiation.

12

Alfonso Bialetti
Espressokocher / espresso maker
Moka Express
1933
Bialetti Industrie S.p.A., Coccaglio, BS
16 x 14,9 x 9 cm
Aluminium / aluminium
Collection Grazyna Ubik

Mit der Espressomaschine *Moka Express* sollte erstmals jedem ermöglicht werden, einen Espresso, wie er bis dahin nur in Bars erhältlich war, auch im privaten Haushalt ohne technische Vorkenntnisse zubereiten zu können. Beim Erhitzen wird das Wasser mit geringem Dampfdruck durch den Kaffee gepresst. Ursprünglich nur in Aluminium gefertigt, hat die „Maschine" ihre charakteristische achteckige Form bis heute beibehalten und wird in verschiedenen Größen angeboten.

With the *Moka Express* espresso machine, coffee lovers could finally prepare professional-quality espresso

in their own home without any special expertise or fancy equipment. Upon being heated, the water is forced through the ground coffee using low vapour pressure. Originally produced in aluminium, the "machine" has retained its distinctive octagonal form and comes in various sizes depending on the required capacity.

13

anonym / anonymous (Japan)
Sandalen / sandals
1. Hälfte 20. Jhdt. / 1st half 20th century
Echigoya, Tokyo
(eine Sandale / one sandal) 12 x 11 x 22 cm
Holz; Leder, gefüttert; Baumwolle; Eisen / wood; leather; cotton; iron
Collection Vitra Design Museum, Weil am Rhein

Die *geta* genannten Holzsandalen sind Teil der traditionellen japanischen Kleidung. Ihre hohen Absätze tragen dem in Japan besonders kultivierten Gebot der Reinlichkeit Rechnung, da sie in erster Linie dazu dienen, die Füße vom Unrat der Straße fernzuhalten.

Geta wooden sandals are part of the traditional dress in Japan. Their elevated platform soles accommodate the well-cultivated Japanese belief in cleanliness by keeping the feet at a safe distance from the filth of the street.

14

Sandalen / sandals
undatiert / undated
Ryohin Keikaku Co. Ltd. (MUJI), Tokyo
5,5 x 30,7 x 11,5 cm (eine Sandale / one sandal)
Polyurethanschaum; TPE / polyurethane foam; TPE
Vitra Design Museum, Weil am Rhein

15

anonym (Frankreich) / anonymous (France)
Pferdedecke des französischen Militärs /
French military horse blanket
ca. 1968
0,4 x 183 x 244 cm
Collection Alexander von Vegesack, Lessac-Confolens

16

Leopold Zacher
Pantoffeln / slippers
undatiert / undated
Zacher Johann & Co. OHG, Innichen / San Candido, Italien
7,5 x 12 x 29,7 cm (ein Pantoffel / one slipper)
Walkfilz
Vitra Design Museum, Weil am Rhein

Zur Herstellung dieser Pantoffeln wird die gewaschene, gekämmte und zum Vlies aufbereitete Rohwolle so lange in Handarbeit über einem Leisten gewalkt, bis die Fasern zu einem einzigen, durchgehenden Stück verfilzt sind, das überall die nötige Dicke und Festigkeit hat.

For the production of these slippers, the raw wool is washed, combed, and processed into fleece, and then felted by hand over a last until the fibres have become matted into a single uniform piece with the correct thickness and consistency throughout.

17

Naoto Hiroka
Pantoffeln / slippers
One Piece Slippers
2004
naoca, Tokyo
5,2 x 11,3 x 26 cm (eine Sandale / one sandal)
Leder / leather
Collection Alexander von Vegesack, Lessac-Confolens

18

T-Shirt
undatiert / undated
RAGMAN, Textilhandel GmbH, Waldshut-Tiengen
84 x 54 x 0,5 cm
Baumwolle / cotton
Collection Mathias Schwartz-Clauss

19

Kleiderbügel / clothes hanger
undatiert / undated
Ryohin Keikaku Co. Ltd. (MUJI), Tokyo
21 x 38 x 0,3 cm
Aluminiumdraht / aluminium-wire
Collection Mathias Schwartz-Clauss

20

Toshiyuki Kita
Ceremony Space
1986
Ohmukai-Kosyudo, Tokyo
180 x 180 x 180 cm
Holz (Urushi-lackiert); Ryukyu Tatami-Matte / wood (urushi-lacquered), ryukyu tatami mat
Collection Alexander von Vegesack, Lessac-Confolens

21

Klistierbirne / enema syringe
undatiert / undated
15 x 7 x 7 cm
Gummi / rubber
Collection Franco Clivio

22

Wasserflasche / water bottle
ca. 1990
32 x 8 x 8 cm
Polyethylenterephthalat (PET)
Collection Mathias Schwartz-Clauss

23

Thermosflasche / thermos bottle
1922
SIGG, Switzerland AG, Frauenfeld
21,5 x 7 x 7 cm
Aluminium, lackiert; Kunststoff; Gummi
Collection Studio 2

24

Naturschwamm / natural sponge
undatiert / undated
(Mittelmeer / Mediterranean)
12 x 19 x 8 cm
Hornkieselschwamm / demosponge
Collection Franco Clivio

Schwämme sind Tiere, die uns – vom Meeresgrund abgetrennt, gereinigt und getrocknet – als fertige Gebrauchsgegenstände dienen. Die elastischen Fasern ermöglichen eine unkomplizierte Variation ihrer Größe, so dass sie für unterschiedlichste Zwecke einsetzbar sind. Sie können beliebig oft große Mengen von Flüssigkeiten aufnehmen und auf kleinstem Raum speichern und geben diese erst unter Druck wieder ab.

Removed from the sea bed, cleaned, and then dried, sponges are animals that provide us with ready-made articles of daily use. The elastic fibres allow for great variation in size, enabling them to be used for all manner of functions. Again and again, they are able to absorb large quantities of liquid and hold them within a compact volume, only releasing them upon being squeezed.

25

anonym / anonymous
Eierkarton / egg carton
undatiert / undated
7 x 10,5 x 15 cm
Pappmaché / papier mâché
Collection Vitra Design Museum, Weil am Rhein

26

anonym / anonymous
Flachmann / hip flask
ca. 1938
11 x 6,4 x 2,2 cm
Silber; Kork / silver; cork
Collection Mathias Schwartz-Clauss

Die leicht gewölbte Form dieses früher als Taschenflasche bezeichneten Gefäßes ist dem Körper angepasst und verstaut so den meist hochprozentigen Proviant ebenso bequem wie unsichtbar unter der Kleidung.

Traditionally referred to as a hip flask, the slightly curved form of this vessel is adapted to the body, allowing the user to carry the typically high-proof contents in comfort and out of view beneath his or her clothing.

27

Schale / bowl
undatiert / undated
Ryohin Keikaku Co. Ltd. (MUJI), Tokyo
7,4 x 12,6 x 12,6 cm
Holz / wood
Collection Mathias Schwartz-Clauss

28

Latex-Kondom / latex condom
Durex
1931 (Markteinführung / commercial launch)
SSL International plc, London
2,5 x 4 x 4 cm
Latex / latex
Collection Vitra Design Museum, Weil am Rhein

Seit 1931 aus flüssigem Naturkautschuk-Latex herge-stellt, zeichnet sich dieses Verhütungsmittel durch hohe Reißfestigkeit und Elastizität aus, obwohl es mit einer Dicke von ca. 0,07 mm etwa sechsmal dünner ist als die menschliche Haut.

Manufactured since 1931 out of liquid natural rubber latex, this contraceptive device is characterized by a high degree of tear resistance and elasticity, despite being only 0.07 millimetre thick—roughly six times thinner than human skin.

29

Beutel mit Druckverschluss /
storage bag with double zipper
ITW Minigrip, Seguin, TX
23 x 17,8 x 0,1 cm
Polyethylen / polyethylene
Collection Vitra Design Museum, Weil am Rhein

Plastikbeutel erfüllen ihre Funktion meist erst dann wirklich sinnvoll, wenn sie auch sicher zu verschließen sind, möglichst sogar luftdicht. Dieser transparente Beutel zeichnet sich durch den patentierten Verschluss aus, der einen flexiblen Gebrauch und die mehrmalige Verwendung erlaubt.

Plastic bags reach their utmost level of functionality when they can be securely closed, ideally with an airtight seal. This transparent bag is distinguished by the patented closure which enables flexible and repeated usage.

30

Paul Schmidt (Erfinder / inventor)
Batterie / battery
1896 (Erfindung / invention)
Alkaline Plus
Duracell, Mönchengladbach
5 x 1,4 x 1,4 cm
verschiedene Materialien / mixed media
Collection Vitra Design Museum, Weil am Rhein

31

Brühwürfel / bouillon cube
1908 (Markteinführung / commercial launch)
Maggi GmbH (Nestlé Deutschland, Frankfurt / Main)
1 x 3 x 2,8 cm
pflanzliches Eiweiß; tierisches Eiweiß; Salz; ca. 300 Geschmacksverstärker und Aluminiumfolie / vegetable protein; animal protein; salt; ca. 300 flavour enhancer and aluminium foil
Collection Vitra Design Museum, Weil am Rhein

32

Compact Disc
(CD-R, 700 MB, 80 min)
1982 (Markteinführung / commercial launch)
Imation, Oakdale, MN
0,1 x 12 x 12 cm
Polycarbonat / polycarbonate
Collection Vitra Design Museum, Weil am Rhein

Auf seiner von innen nach außen laufenden Spiralspur mit einer Gesamtlänge von etwa 6 km kann dieses optische Medium hohe Datenmengen speichern, die von einem Laser abgetastet und dadurch gelesen werden können. Die CD wurde gemeinsam von den Firmen Philips und Sony entwickelt und 1981 in einer BBC-Fernsehsendung mit einem Song der Bee Gees erstmals vorgestellt. Ihr standardisierter Durchmesser von 12 cm entspricht einer Vorgabe der Produzenten, wonach sie in jede An-zugtasche passen sollte.

On its spiral track running centrifugally to a total length of about 6 kilometres, this optical medium stores large amounts of data that can be scanned and read by a laser. The CD was jointly developed by Philips and Sony and made its public debut in 1981 with a recording of the Bee Gees on BBC TV. The rationale behind its standardized diameter of 12 centimetres is that it be small enough to fit into a jacket pocket.

33

Kreditkarte / credit card
1950er Jahre / 1950s
0,1 x 5,4 x 8,5 cm
Collection Mathias Schwartz-Clauss

Kreditkarten machten aus dem universalen Zahlungs- und Tauschmittel Geld eine noch abstraktere Größe. Weltweit einsetzbar bieten sie nicht nur einen zeitlich und räumlich erweiterten finanziellen Spielraum, sondern auch mehr Platz in der Tasche. Ihre Form und Abmessungen sind international verbindlich in der ISO-Norm 7810 festgelegt (ISO: International Organization for Standardization).

As a universal means of payment and exchange, money is endowed with an even greater abstract quality through credit cards. Usable worldwide, they not only offer ex-panded financial flexibility in time and space but also more room in the pocket. Their shape and size are specified by the internationally binding ISO 7810 standard.

34

Jules Poupitch
Multipack Carrier
Side Applied Multipack, 6-Pack
1958
Hi-Cone, Itasca, IL
0,01 x 22,3 x 11,2 cm
LDPE photodegradable plastic (Polyethylen / polyethylene)
Collection Vitra Design Museum, Weil am Rhein

Dieses weltweite Verpackungspatent bietet maximale Funktionalität bei minimalem Materialaufwand. Die transparente Folie mit runden Ausstanzungen, die bis zu zwölf Dosen oder Flaschen sicher hält, sorgt nicht nur für Effizienz bei Transport und Lagerung, sondern rückt vor allem das Produkt und nicht die Verpackung in den Vordergrund. Überdies wird der anfallende Müll erheblich reduziert.

This worldwide patented packaging device offers maxi-mum functionality through minimal expenditure of material. Able to secure up to twelve cans or bottles, the transparent plastic film with round cut-outs not only ensures efficiency in transport and storage but also brings the product and not the packaging to the fore. In addition, the resulting waste is considerably less than with any other alternatives.

35

Diamant / diamond
2008
0,5 x 0,5 x 0,5 cm
Kohlenstoff, geschliffen / polished carbon
Boghossian SA, Genève

36

Shiro Kuramata
Miniatur nach dem Originalentwurf von 1976 / miniature of the original of 1976
Glass Chair
16,8 x 16 x 11,5 cm
Glas / glass
Collection Alexander von Vegesack, Lessac-Confolens

37

Taschenbuch / pocketbook
Homer: Odyssee / Odyssey
Reclams Universal-Bibliothek, Nr. 280
2009 (1. Aufl. 1979)
Philipp Reclam jun. GmbH & Co., Stuttgart
14,8 x 9,6 x 2 cm
Papier / paper
Collection Vitra Design Museum, Weil am Rhein

Reclam-Hefte sind die Bücher der sogenannten *Univer-sal-Bibliothek* des 1828 in Leipzig gegründeten Reclam Verlages. Die Sammlung internationaler Literatur begann 1867 und umfasst heute über 20 000 Bände, die durch ihre äußerst sparsame Ausstattung im Taschenbuchfor-mat Bildung für alle zu einem geringen Preis zugänglich machen.

Reclam books are the small-format volumes of the *Universal-Bibliothek* ("Universal Library") of the Reclam publishing house founded in Leipzig in 1828. This collection of international literature began in 1867 and today encompasses more than 20,000 books, whose economical layout in paperback format makes the literary world available to all at a modest price.

38

William Middlebrook (Erfinder / inventor)
industriell gefertigte Büroklammer / industrially manufactured paper clip
1890 (Erfindung / invention)
Ryohin Keikaku Co. Ltd. (MUJI), Tokyo
0 x 2,8 x 0,7 cm
Metalldraht / metal wire
Collection Vitra Design Museum, Weil am Rhein

1899 erhielt der Amerikaner William Middlebrook das Patent für die industrielle Fertigung von Büroklammern. Nur aus einem Metalldraht gebogen, halten sie je nach Größe eine Vielzahl von Blättern zusammen, ohne sie dauerhaft zu fixieren.

In 1899, the American William Middlebrook obtained the patent for the industrial manufacture of paper clips. Bent from a single piece of metal wire, they bind together multiple pages without permanently attaching one to the other and come in various sizes to accommodate different volumes of paper.

39

Dreispitz-Reißnagel / tricorn drawing pin
Omega
1947
Lüdi Swiss AG, Flawil
0,5 x 1,5 x 1,5 cm
Stahl / steel
Collection Vitra Design Museum, Weil am Rhein

40

Klebezettel / adhesive label
Post-it
1974
3M, Neuss, Deutschland
1 x 7,6 x 7,6 cm
Papier; Klebstoff / paper; glue
Collection Vitra Design Museum, Weil am Rhein

Im Jahr 1968 entdeckte der bei dem Technologieunter-nehmen 3M (Minnesota Mining and Manufacturing Company) angestellte Chemiker Spencer Silver zufällig einen nur leicht haftenden Kleber, der zur Grundlage für die Entwicklung des *Post-it* wurde, die sein Kollege Art Fry bis zur Markteinführung im Jahr 1977 vorantrieb. Durch die reduzierte Klebekraft der quadratischen Zettel können Notizen auf fast allen Oberflächen angebracht und nahezu rückstandsfrei wieder entfernt werden.

In 1968, Spencer Silver, a chemist at the 3M technology company (Minnesota Mining and Manufacturing Company), accidentally discovered a low-tack adhesive that provided the basis for the development of the Post-it, which was further developed and refined by his colleague Art Fry up to its initial market launch in 1977. The reduced adhesive strength of the square slips of paper allows notes to be stuck on almost all surfaces and later removed with virtually no residue.

41

Maßband / measuring tape
undatiert / undated
Prym Consumer GmbH, Stollberg
0,1 x 150 x 1,9 cm
Kunststoff; Metall / plastic; metal
Collection Mathias Schwartz-Clauss

42

anonym (Deutschland) / anonymous (Germany)
Faden auf Spule mit Nähnadel /
spool of thread with sewing needle
1980
3,3 x 2,7 x 2,7 cm
Ahornholz; Baumwolle und Edelstahl / maple wood;
cotton and stainless steel
Collection Mathias Schwartz-Clauss

Eines der ältesten Handwerkzeuge, das bei minimaler Größe eine maximale Wirkung entfaltet.

One of the oldest manual tools, maximum effect is achieved here with minimal size.

43

anonym (Skandinavien) / anonymous (Scandinavia)
Schneebesen / egg whip
undatiert / undated
4,5 x 29,5 x 5,7 cm
Holz / wood
Collection Franco Clivio

Dieses Küchenwerkzeug aus Skandinavien besteht aus einem einzigen, mit einem Vierkantholz verklebten Holzstreifen, dessen Torsion Flüssigkeiten beim Schlagen zusätzlich verwirbelt.

This kitchen utensil from Scandinavia consists of a rectangular wooden handle bonded with a single flexible strip of wood whose torsion helps to swirl ingredients when beating liquids.

44

anonym / anonymous (Japan)
Essstäbchen / chopsticks
ca. 1990
0,6 x 25,7 x 1 cm
Holz / wood
Collection Alexander von Vegesack, Lessac-Confolens

45

Alfred Neweczerzal
Sparschäler / peeler
Rex
1947
Zena AG, Affoltern a. A.
1,3 x 11,1 x 6,6 cm
Stahl, vernickelt; Eisen / steel, nickel-plated; iron
Collection Vitra Design Museum, Weil am Rhein

Diesem Gerät ist nichts hinzuzufügen: Die Form des Bügels entspricht der Haltung der Hand, die beweglich gelagerte Schneide samt Abstandhalter verhindert zu tiefes Abschälen und eine Öse am Ende dient zum Ausstechen schlechter Stellen.

This device is hard to improve upon: the form of the U-shaped handle fits the clasp of the hand, the flexible blade and spacer prevent the user from cutting too deeply, and a loop affixed to the side serves to excise blemishes.

46

anonym / anonymous (Japan)
Schere / scissors
undatiert / undated
1 x 12,1 x 2,7 cm
Eisen / iron
Collection Franco Clivio

47

anonym / anonymous (Mali)
Faustkeil / hand axe
Altsteinzeit / Palaeolithic
6,5 x 21 x 9 cm (9,6 kg)
Quarzit / quartzite
Collection Strüker, Basel

Aufgrund ihrer zahlreichen Funktionen wie Schneiden, Schaben, Schlagen oder Werfen werden die meist ovalen oder konisch geformten Werkzeuge auch als „Schweizer Messer der Steinzeit" bezeichnet. Gefertigt wurden sie vor ca. 1,5 Mio. Jahren erstmals in Afrika durch das Abtragen des Materials vom Ursprungsstein.

Due to its multiple functions, such as cutting, scraping, striking, or tossing, these typically oval or conically shaped tools are also referred to as the "Swiss Army knives of the Stone Age". They were first fabricated about 1.5 million years ago in Africa by flaking away pieces of the original stone.

48

Topfuntersetzer / pot mat
undatiert / undated
1,5 x 18 x 18 cm
Edelstahl / stainless steel
Collection Franco Clivio

49

Giulio Iacchetti; Matteo Ragni
Göffel / spork
Moscardino
2000
Pandora Design
7,9 x 4 x 1,5 cm
Plastik / plastic
Collection Mathias Schwartz-Clauss

Der Göffel ist eine Kombination aus Gabel und Löffel. Bereits 1583 vom deutschen Instrumentenmacher Christoph Trechsler erfunden, kam das Prinzip erst Ende des 20. Jahrhunderts in Mode. Während üblicherweise die Löffelschale um Gabelzinken erweitert wird, liegen sich hier Löffel und Gabel gegenüber, wobei – gerade noch bequem zu handhaben – der eine Teil jeweils als Griff für den anderen dient.

The spork is a combination of fork and spoon. Invented back in 1583 by the German instrument maker Christoph Trechsler, the principle was not embraced by the public until the late twentieth century. Typically, the bowl of the spoon is extended with fork tines, but here the spoon and fork are at opposite ends with one part serving as the handle of the other, leaving something to be desired as far as ease of handling is concerned.

50

Klapp-Rasierer / foldable razor
undatiert / undated
El Berel Italiana
2,5 x 4,3 x 9,3 cm (gefaltet / folded: 0,8 x 4,3 x 4,3 cm)
Kunststof; Edelstahl / plastic; stainless steel
Collection Studio 2

51

Wil Offermans
Flöte / recorder
Thumpy
1997
2,3 x 39,5 x 2,3 cm
Ahornholz / maple wood
Collection Mathias Schwartz-Clauss

52

Toilettenpapierrolle / toilet paper roll
2. Hälfte 19. Jhdt. / 2nd half 19th century
(Erfindung / invention)
Edeka AG & Co. KG, Hamburg
9,5 x 12,5 x 12,5 cm
Papier / paper
Collection Vitra Design Museum, Weil am Rhein

Trotz seines einfachen Aufbaus muss dieser Hygiene-artikel vielen Anforderungskriterien genügen, zu denen sowohl gute Griffigkeit, Reißfestigkeit und Portionier-barkeit als auch Haltbarkeit und leichte Zersetzbarkeit gehören.

In 1928, the Hakle company intoduced the first toilet paper in roll form to European markets. Despite its simple design, this hygiene article needs to satisfy numerous requirements, including a good grip, tearing resistance, and portionability, as well as long storage life and ease of decomposition.

53

Stephen Perry (Erfinder / inventor)
Gummiband / rubber band)
1845 (Erfindung / invention)
0,4 x 12 x 5 cm
Gummi / rubber
Collection Vitra Design Museum, Weil am Rhein

54

Heinrich Wöhlk (Erfinder / inventor)
luftdurchlässige, harte Kontaktlinse /
rigid gas permeable contact lens
1976 (Markteinführung / commercial launch)
Hecht Contactlinsen GmbH, Freiburg
0,1 x 1 x 1 cm
Boston ES©-Polymer
Collection Vitra Design Museum, Weil am Rhein

55

anonym / anonymous (Japan)
Fächer / fan
undatiert / undated
2 x 40 x 27,5 cm
Holz; Papier; Eisen; Lack / wood; paper; iron; lacquer
Collection Franco Clivio

Mathias Schwartz-Clauss

DIE ESSENZ DER DINGE – DESIGN UND DIE KUNST DER REDUKTION /
THE ESSENCE OF THINGS – DESIGN AND THE ART OF REDUCTION

Hannes Meyer, *Co-op* Interieur, Basel 1926. „Objets-types" für die „Halbnomaden des heutigen Wirtschaftslebens", unbekannter Fotograf (Hannes Meyer), gta Archiv, ETH Zürich, Nachlass Hannes Meyer.

Hannes Meyer, *Co-op* Interior, Basle 1926. "Objets-types" for the "semi-nomads of current economic life", photographer unknown (Hannes Meyer), gta Archiv, ETH Zürich, Nachlass Hannes Meyer.

Die einfachste Lösung zu suchen ist eine Triebfeder menschlichen Handelns, denn in all unseren Weltverhältnissen wollen wir Komplexität auf Prinzipien, Begriffe und praktische Lösungen reduzieren: in Religionen, die durch ihre normative Kraft einen einenden Sinn und Wege zum „richtigen" Leben verheißen, in Wissenschaften, die nach objektiven Regeln für natürliche und gesellschaftliche Phänomene forschen und diese in Theorien fassen, im Rechtswesen, das für das menschliche Zusammenleben verbindliche Gesetze festlegt, und in den Künsten, die versuchen, Erlebnissen, Gefühlen und Gedanken eine fassliche Gestalt zu geben. Formulierungen schätzen wir umso mehr, je treffsicherer sie ihren Gegenstand auf den Punkt bringen, und weil diese Abstraktionsleistung eine so grundlegende Eigenschaft unseres Intellekts ist, sind wir geneigt, unser ganzes Tun daran zu messen, wie erfolgreich diese Strategie angewandt wird. Dass diese Leistung besonders dort gefordert ist, wo Nützliches gestaltet werden soll, liegt geradezu auf der Hand.

Reduktion ist also auch im Design ein Grundsatz. Aber um etwas als komplex oder einfach einzustufen, braucht man einen Bezugsrahmen, denn eine minimalistische Gestalt allein zeigt noch nicht, ob tatsächlich nach der Maxime *Less is more*[1] auch gestaltet wurde. Design ist, wie George Nelson sagt, „ein vollständiger Ausdruck dessen, was ein Ding ist oder tut",[2] und so gehört es ebenfalls zu den Aufgaben des Designers, den Aufwand an Materialien, Werkzeugen und Arbeit sowie den für die Logistik von Verpackung, Lagerung und Transport einzukalkulieren. Unterschlagen wird oft auch der Aufwand, den die Ideenfindung selbst mit sich bringt, wofür wieder andere Entwürfe, Vorbilder wichtig sein können. All diese Faktoren fließen in die Gestaltung von Produkten und schließlich in die ihres Preises – der eine weitere Funktion ist – mit ein. Wenn man dazu noch Emotionen und Botschaften zählt, die ein Objekt vermitteln soll, wird es fast unmöglich, angemessen zu beurteilen, ob ein Entwurf im Sinne der Reduktion auch gelungen ist.

Vor allem die Gefühle müssen ins Feld geführt werden, um zu verstehen, warum trotz der Vorzüge einer rein funktionalen Gestaltung dieses Prinzip so oft widerlegt wird. Denn ein „guter" Gegenstand ist offenbar einer, von dem wir mehr erwarten als nur das zuverlässige Funktionieren. Wo Konsum als wichtiger Bestandteil der Lebensqualität empfunden wird, fallen die meisten Kaufentscheidungen nicht etwa danach, was gebraucht wird, sondern danach, was Gefühle kurzfristig befriedigt. Der von Karl Marx beschriebene „Fetischcharakter der Ware"[3] zeigt sich vielleicht an Objekten mit „Design"-Label besonders deutlich. Viele Wohnungen spiegeln deshalb schnelllebige Modeeinflüsse oder die Unsicherheit ihrer Bewohner und gleichen einer „ungeheuren Warensammlung"[4], die so gut wie nie benutzt wird. Und selbst der vornehme Minimalismus eleganter Apartments, in denen nur wahrer Kunst das Wort erteilt wird, ist oft bloß eine Kulisse, hinter der das Chaos des Alltags versteckt wird.

Finding the simplest solution to a problem is one of the driving forces of human action. In our relationship with the world, we seek to reduce complexity to principles, concepts, and practical solutions. Thus, religions promise, through their normative power, a unifying purpose and pathways towards the "right" way of life; science searches for the objective rules that underlie natural and social phenomena and articulates them in theories; legal systems establish laws to govern human coexistence; the arts attempt to give tangible form to experiences, feelings, and thoughts. The more aptly they capture the subject at hand, the greater their resonance and appeal. Because abstraction is such a fundamental characteristic of our intellect, we are inclined to measure all we do against how successfully it is applied. And in this respect, the design of essentials is hardly an exception, for the act of abstraction seems especially imperative to it.

Reduction is hence also a basic principle in design. Yet in order to classify something as complex or simple, a frame of reference is needed, for minimalist form alone does not fully indicate whether it was truly designed according to the maxim of Less is More.[1] As articulated by George Nelson, design is "a full expression of what a thing is or does",[2] and a designer's job thus includes taking into account materials, tools, and labour, as well as the logistics of packaging, storage, and transport. The effort involved in generating the idea itself, for which other designs and models can in turn be important, is often left unmentioned. All these factors are incorporated in the product and ultimately in its pricing as well, which operates as a further function. Adding in the emotions and messages one hopes to express through the object, it becomes almost impossible to assess whether a design has succeeded with respect to reduction.

In particular, the role of emotions needs to be acknowledged in order to understand why the principle of reduction is so frequently refuted despite the advantages of purely functional design. For a "good" object is apparently one from which we expect more than just reliable functionality. In an age when consumption is perceived as an important component of quality of life, purchasing decisions are typically based not on need but on immediate emotional gratification. The "fetishism of the world of commodities"[3] described by Karl Marx is perhaps especially apparent in objects bearing the "design" label. Many living spaces hence reflect the influence of fast-changing fashions and respectively the insecurity of their occupants, evincing an "immense collection of commodities"[4] scarcely ever subjected to actual use. And even the noble mini-

Die Kargheit dieser asketischen Räume ist bewusst gewählt und aufgeladen mit der Überlegenheitsgeste vornehmen Verzichts, der Konzentration auf das Wesentliche und, vielleicht, der Erwartung einer Erleuchtung. Während hier jedoch die Leere des Raumes eine Elite ausweist, die international dieselbe Sprache spricht, kennzeichnet sie andernorts die blanke Not. In diesem Spannungsfeld zeigen sich auch die Bandbreite und Komplexität einer zeitgemäßen Überlegung zur Reduktion in der Gestaltung: Ob es sich um Luxus, Armut oder Askese handelt, um Verzicht als Variante des Überflusses, um Entbehrung, etwa unter Bedingungen von Haft, um Enthaltsamkeit als spirituelle Haltung im Kloster oder spartanische Strenge als totalitäre Unterdrückung – die Semantik reduzierter Formen ergibt sich vor allem aus dem Kontext, in dem sie uns erscheinen.

Die Frage stellt sich mithin nach einem goldenen Mittelweg, dem vernünftigen Maß als einem Ideal von Reduktion, nach dem kleinsten gemeinsamen Nenner geschichtlicher Entwicklungen oder nach jener Schnittmenge aus Gefühl und Verstand, die lang anhaltende Zufriedenheit mit den Dingen verspricht. Hier suchen wir nach etwas, das sich vielleicht in der Lebenswelt der Shaker verkörpert, jener religiösen Gemeinschaft von Handwerkern und Bauern in Amerika, die fern des im 19. Jahrhundert einsetzenden Konsumter-

rors eins mit sich und der Welt ihr Tagwerk verrichteten und ihre Häuser mit Dingen ausstatteten, die nicht hinterfragt zu werden brauchten, solange sie ihren Dienst taten.[5] Nach dieser Art von Gegenständen und dieser Art des Umgangs mit ihnen – denn das eine lässt sich vom andern nicht trennen – suchen wir, unter wechselnden Vorzeichen, seitdem wir gemerkt haben, dass sie uns abhanden gekommen sind.

Vielleicht ist Reduktion überhaupt das falsche Stichwort, um manche Schöpfung zu verstehen, an die wir hier denken, weil da nichts weggenommen und nichts abstrahiert wurde, sondern es eigentlich um einen Neuanfang geht. Die Befreiung von (lokalen) Traditionen und das Streben nach (universeller) Revolution begleiten die Moderne seitdem sie sich der Herrschaft der Vernunft und dem künstlerischen Genie als Vollender der Natur verschrieben hatte. Die aus klaren geometrischen Grundformen geschnittenen Monumentalbauten der so genannten Revolutionsarchitektur in Frankreich, deren eindrucksvollste Entwürfe Visionen blieben, fanden den radikalsten Ausdruck dafür. Etienne-Louis Boullées 1784 gezeichneter *Isaac-Newton-Kenotaph*, der das Weltall ins Innere einer gigantischen Kugel kehrt und von außen einen Planeten darstellt, wollte mit dieser kühnen Demonstration von Geometrie einen Wissenschaftler ehren, der davon überzeugt war, dass man „Wahr-

malism of elegant apartments, in which only true art enjoys pride of place, often turns out to be a mere backdrop concealing the chaos of daily life.

The starkness of these ascetic interiors is a deliberate choice—a superiority-signalling gesture of lofty renunciation, of concentration on the essential, and, perhaps, of an expectation of enlightenment. While such emptiness of space signifies an elite that speaks the same coded international language, elsewhere it means sheer hardship and deprivation. Such contrasts and tensions demonstrate clearly the scope and complexity of a present-day consideration of reduction in design. Whether a matter of luxury, poverty, or asceticism—of refusal as a variant of excess, of deprivation as found under conditions of imprisonment, of abstention as a monastic disciplin, or of Spartan austerity as

totalitarian oppression—the semantics of reduced forms emerge first and foremost from the context in which they appear.

The question of a golden mean therefore presents itself—a reasonable measure as an ideal of reduction, a lowest common denominator of historical developments, or an intersection of sense and sensibility that promises enduring satisfaction with objects. Here we are seeking something that seems to have been embodied in the world of the nineteenth-century Shakers, the American religious community of craftsmen and farmers that went about their daily tasks at one with themselves and the world. Deliberately distanced from the oppressive consumerism that had taken hold, they outfitted their homes with things that did not need to be questioned as long as they performed

their intended task.[5] Such types of objects and such a manner of dealing with them—for the one is inseparable from the other—are what we have been seeking, under changing circumstances, ever since the realization that these objects and ways of life have slipped away from us.

Reduction might even be the wrong word as far as some of the creations alluded to are concerned, for nothing has been taken away from them and nothing has been abstracted. Rather, they have to do with a new beginning. The liberation from (local) traditions and the quest for (universal) revolution have accompanied the modern era ever since it embraced the rule of reason and crowned artistic genius as the consummator of nature. The most radical expression of this can be found in the clear-cut geometric shapes of the monumental buildings of so-called revolution-

heit stets in der Einfachheit und nicht in der Vielfalt und Unordnung der Dinge findet"[6].

Die Anfänge der Geometrie liegen selbst in einer Art von Reduktion: in der Vermessung der Natur und ihrer Abstraktion, aus der eine eigene Logik entwickelt wurde. Als Alexander von Humboldt von 1845 bis 1862 als Letzter den Versuch einer umfassenden physischen Weltbeschreibung mit seinem Monumentalwerk *Kosmos* unternahm und formulierte „Die Natur ist für die denkende Betrachtung Einheit in der Vielheit, Verbindung des Mannigfaltigen in Form und Mischung, Inbegriff der Naturdinge und Naturkräfte, als ein lebendiges Ganze"[7], beschrieb Charles Darwin die Entstehung der Arten nicht als fortschreitende Perfektionierung, sondern als gesetzmäßige Ausdifferenzierung durch Anpassung und natürliche Zuchtwahl. Mit diesen Forschungen im Geiste der Aufklärung ging das „Postulat der Gesetzmäßigkeit als eines einfachen Grundsatzes [...] auf die Erforschung des Lebens über"[8], und was diese Theorien beschreiben – in den Natur- wie in den Gesellschaftswissenschaften –, ist eine immer weitere Differenzierung. Die wissenschaftlichen Modelle streben also nach Abstraktion und Vereinfachung, die Welt wird derweil aber immer komplexer und komplizierter.

Und so ursprünglich wie in den Gesetzmäßigkeiten der Natur erscheint uns Einfachheit auch in den Anfängen unserer Kultur, von primitiven Faustkeilen bis zu den Bauten der frühen Hochkulturen, wobei erst die Anwendung der Gesetze von Mathematik und Statik sowie die Nutzung rationaler Arbeitsteilung und gesellschaftlicher Hierarchien monumentale Werke wie die Pyramiden ermöglichten.[9]

Die Komplexität des Einfachen oder die Einfachheit des Komplexen, die gegenseitige Spiegelung und Steigerung von Schlichtem und Großem sowie von Kompliziertem und Kleinem ist ein wiederkehrendes Motiv in bildender und angewandter Kunst der Moderne. Am Vorabend der Industrialisierung beschrieb Johann Joachim Winckelmann, der Begründer der wissenschaftlichen Kunstgeschichte, das „Idealschöne", das er in der griechisch-antiken Baukunst und Skulptur sah, als „edle Einfalt und stille Größe" – eine ästhetische Einschätzung, die bis heute auch als moralischer Appell verstanden wird. Wir begegnen diesem paradox scheinenden Anspruch im symmetrisch gespiegelten Edelholzfurnier einfacher Biedermeiermöbel ebenso wie in der aus einem Granitblock gehauenen, spiegelglatt polierten Riesenschale von Christian Gottlieb Cantian, die Karl Friedrich Schinkel vor sein Altes Museum in Berlin stellen ließ, in den glasklaren Kompositionen Caspar David Friedrichs, die uns die Vergänglichkeit vor Augen halten, oder im Tod des Revolutionärs Marat in der Badewanne auf dem Bild von Jacques-Louis David. Im 20. Jahrhundert begegnet es uns wieder in Kasimir Malewitschs leicht verrücktem *Schwarzen Quadrat auf weißem Grund*, auf den samtweichen Betonwänden der Bauten Tadao Andos oder heute im intuitiv funktionierenden Interface eines iPod.

----

ary architecture in France, whose most impressive designs did not progress beyond the drawing board. An example in point is the bold demonstration of geometry in Etienne-Louis Boullée's 1784 proposal for a cenotaph for Isaac Newton. In his sketch of the cenotaph, Boullée transferred the heavens onto the inner surface of a gigantic sphere that from the outside depicted a planet, thus seeking to honour a scientist who was convinced that "[t]ruth is ever to be found in simplicity, and not in the multiplicity and confusion of things".[6]

The beginnings of geometry itself lie in a type of reduction: in the measurement of nature and its abstraction, from which an intrinsic logic was developed. In his ultimate attempt to articulate a comprehensive physical description of the world, Alexander von Humboldt wrote—in his monumental work *Cosmos*, printed in multiple volumes from 1845 to 1862—that "[n]ature considered *rationally*, that is to say, submitted to the process of thought, is a unity in diversity of phenomena; a harmony, blending together all created things, however dissimilar in form and attributes; one great whole animated by the breath of life."[7] At the same time, Charles Darwin described the origin of species not as a course of progressive perfection but as a process of differentiation following the laws of adaptation and natural selection. With these investigations embodying the spirit of Enlightenment, the "axiom of the power of laws as a simple principle … was applied to the investigation of life",[8] yet what these theories describe— in both the natural and social sciences— is in fact an evergreater differentiation. The scientific models thus strive for abstraction and simplification while the real world grows more and more complex and complicated.

As basic and primal as in the laws of nature, simplicity also appears in the incipient stages of our culture, from primitive hand axes up to the constructions of early civilizations. This includes monumental buildings like the pyramids, which only became possible through the application of the laws of mathematics and statics and the practice of a rational division of labour and social hierarchies.[9]

The complexity of the simple or the simplicity of the complex, the reciprocal reflection and escalation of unadorned and large, on one hand, and complicated and small, on the other, forms a recurring motif in the fine and applied arts of the modern era. On the eve of industrialization, Johann Joachim Winckelmann, the father of the discipline of art history, described the "ideal beauty" he saw in ancient Greek architecture and sculpture as "noble simplicity and quiet grandeur"—an aesthetic assessment that to this day remains equally understood as a moral appeal. We encounter this seemingly paradoxical

In einer Welt, deren Dichte und Komplexität immer bedrängender werden, sind Vereinfachung und Reduktion demnach zentrale Anliegen. Die Formulierungen, die das industrielle Design dafür gefunden hat, wurden jedoch, so unsere These, von Faktoren bestimmt, die an sich schon von ihren eigenen Widersprüchen geprägt sind: vom technischen Fortschritt, von der modernen Kunst, die die rasanten gesellschaftlichen Veränderungen spiegelt, und vom Einfluss der traditionellen japanischen Kultur.

FERTIGUNG UND LOGISTIK

Die ersten mit Maschinen seriell gefertigten Möbel verbargen noch ihre industrielle Herkunft und entsprachen stilistisch ganz dem Eklektizismus ihrer Zeit. Maschinen sollten – nur eben effizienter als das Handwerk – das produzieren, was gewünscht war – und seien es „gotische Ornamente in Kunststein"[10]. Ein reiner Funktionalismus als Konzentrat aus ökonomischer Produktion und Gebrauchswert fand sich zu Beginn der Industrialisierung nur bei solchen Objekten, die keinem Vorläufer abgeschaut waren: bei Autos, zum Beispiel, elektrischen Geräten oder den Produktionsmaschinen selbst.

Heutige Maschinen bringen die komplexesten Formen hervor und kombinieren unter-

schiedliche Herstellungsprozesse derart, dass Material und Endprodukt mitunter gleichzeitig entstehen. Sie können gar so programmiert werden, dass jedes einzelne Produkt anders aussieht. Diese Industrieproduktion folgt strikt der Logik der Effizienz. Das bedeutet ein hohes Maß an Arbeitsteilung und Kompatibilität zwischen den Akteuren – vom Auftraggeber, Finanzier und Verkäufer über den Designer beziehungsweise Ingenieur bis hin zu den produzierenden Arbeitern und den Maschinen. Schon hinsichtlich der Kommunikation dieser Beteiligten ist eine Vereinfachung von Ideen, Formen und Prozessen von Vorteil. Vor allem aber muss man die Eigenschaften der zu verarbeitenden Materialien mit einkalkulieren. Schließlich sind Gegenstände aus wenigen Materialien und einfachen, standardisierten sowie austauschbaren Teilen mit geraden Umrissen und ebenen Oberflächen in aller Regel effizienter herzustellen – wobei eine Einheit durch Gleichförmigkeit im Gesetz der Serie selbst begründet liegt.

Die schlichten, ganz auf Funktionen zugeschnittenen Formen, wie sie am Ende der Produktionskette stehen, verraten jedoch nichts über den Aufwand, den die Industrie betreibt, um zu derart ökonomischen Lösungen zu kommen. Als erfolgreichstes Produkt der Möbelgeschichte ist dafür Thonets Bugholzstuhl *Nr.*

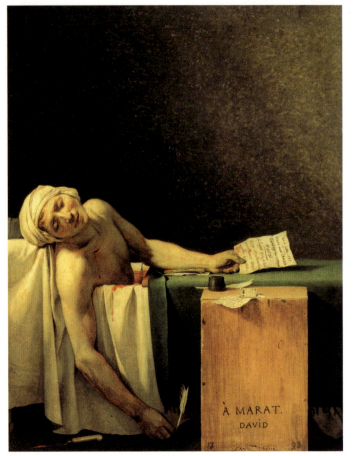

Jacques-Louis David, *La mort de Marat* (Der Tod des Marat), 1793, Öl auf Leinwand, 162 × 128 cm, Königliche Museen der Schönen Künste, Brüssel.

Jacques-Louis David, *La mort de Marat* (The Death of Marat), 1793, oil on canvas, 162 × 128 cm, Royal Museums of Fine Arts of Belgium, Brussels.

standard in the symmetrically mirrored wood veneer of simple Biedermeier furniture as well as in the massive, smoothly polished bowl chiselled from a single block of granite by Christian Gottlieb Cantian and placed by Karl Friedrich Schinkel in front of his Altes Museum in Berlin. We find it in the crystal clear compositions of Caspar David Friedrich, which keep us mindful of ephemerality, and in the bathtub death of the revolutionary figure Marat painted by Jacques-Louis David. In the twentieth century, we come across it yet again in Kasimir Malevich's slightly distorted *Black Square on a White Field*, in the velvety smooth concrete walls of buildings by Tadao Ando, or, today, in the intuitively operated interface of an iPod.

In a world increasingly besieged by density and complexity, simplicity and reduction thus emerge as central

concerns. Yet, according to the following thesis, the formulations supplied by industrial design have been determined by factors that have their own intrinsically defining contradictions: by technological progress, by modern art reflecting the rapid changes in society, and by the influence of traditional Japanese culture.

MANUFACTURING AND LOGISTICS

The first works of furniture serially produced by machines kept their industrial heritage hidden, stylistically corresponding to the broad eclecticism of their day. Factories simply produced what was desired—just more efficiently

than by hand—even if it meant "the moulding of Gothic ornament by machine".[10] In the early stages of industrialization, pure functionalism as a concentration of economic production and utility value was limited to objects that had not been patterned on any predecessors, such as automobiles, electrical devices, or the production machines themselves.

Modern-day machines render forms of utmost complexity and combine various manufacturing processes so that the materials and final product can be created simultaneously. They can even be programmed to make each individual product look different. This mode of industrial production adheres to a strict logic of efficiency. It entails an extensive division of labour and compatibility between the various agents—from the initiator, financier, and retailer to the designer or engineer and on up to the

14 ein gutes Beispiel. Arbeitsteilig in großer Serie vorgefertigt für die Lagerhaltung eines weltweiten Vertriebsnetzes ist dieses Möbel die bis heute vorbildliche Quintessenz eines komplexen technischen Entwicklungsprozesses, der von den Qualitäten des Rohstoffs (der Biegsamkeit und Stabilität von Buchenholz) ausging und einen auf viele Millionen Stühle umzurechnenden Produktionsaufwand konsequent reduzierte. Entscheidend war dabei nicht zuletzt Thonets Rationalisierung der gesamten Logistik – von eigenen Buchenwäldern, Fabriken und Arbeitersiedlungen, die in der Nähe der Wälder aus firmeneigenen Steinen errichtet wurden, über die Publikation mehrsprachiger Verkaufskataloge für ein ständig erweitertes Sortiment bis hin zum weltweiten Versand der Stühle in Einzelteilen an Thonets Vertretungen in den Geschäftszentren der Metropolen. Das Unternehmen nahm damit schon im 19. Jahrhundert die Strategien des heutigen Marktführers IKEA vorweg. Gemeinsam ist beiden Konzepten das Ziel der Kostenersparnis, und beide prägten mit ihren Produkten über Generationen die Einrichtung: Während Thonets Abstraktionen von Biedermeier-Entwürfen eine schlichte, leicht zu handhabende Massenmöblierung ermöglichten, verkörpern IKEAs einfache Formen und Farben ein typisch skandinavi-

sches Image von Solidität, das sich den weltweit unterschiedlichen Vorlieben gegenüber neutral verhält.

Wie diffizil es sich im Industriedesign mit der Ökonomie verhält, zeigt sich nicht zuletzt darin, dass der Entwicklungsaufwand für ein Produkt und die Investitionen ins Fabrikationswerkzeug mit Kosten verbunden sind, die sich erst im Verlauf der Verkäufe amortisieren. So rechnete sich auch das „Prinzip Thonet" nur über die enormen Stückzahlen. Wenn sich aber die Rahmenbedingungen ändern, Patente auslaufen, neue Technologien und Konkurrenten auf den Markt kommen oder eine Wirtschaftskrise die Kaufkraft lähmt, ändert sich auch die Rentabilität. Der traditionsreiche Glashersteller Iittala etwa, der in den 1930er Jahren mit Aino Aaltos Entwürfen berühmt wurde, hatte Mitte der 1990er Jahre eine Produktpalette von 15 000 Modellen und schrumpfte diese auf mittlerweile etwa 3000 gesund, wobei er seinen Umsatz noch enorm steigern konnte. Und wo früher der Designer seinen Gewinn vor allem mit den *royalties* industrieller Serienprodukte erzielte, verdient er heute oft mehr mit handgefertigten Prototypen, die ohne Folgeproduktion bleiben. Hier schließt sich der Kreislauf einer Entwicklung im Design, die zu Beginn der Indu-

Tadao Ando,
Vitra Konferenzpavillon, 1993,
Foto: Thomas Dix, Vitra.

Tadao Ando,
Vitra Conference Pavillon, 1993,
photograph: Thomas Dix, Vitra.

manufacturing workers and machines. Even in the communication between these participants, a simplification of ideas, forms, and processes is advantageous. Above all, however, one must take into account the properties of the materials being processed. Objects made of few materials and simple, standardized, and interchangeable parts, with straight contours and flat surfaces, can generally be manufactured more efficiently—whereby unity through uniformity is rooted in the law of serial production itself.

Nevertheless, the simple forms tailored to specific functions that emerge at the end of the production chain reveal nothing about the effort and expense undertaken by industry to arrive at such economical solutions. The most successful product in furniture history, Thonet's bentwood chair *No. 14*, provides a good

example of this rule. Prefabricated on a large scale employing a division of labour to supply the warehouses of a worldwide distribution network, this piece of furniture exemplifies the quintessence of a complex technical development process based on the qualities of the raw material (the pliability and stability of beechwood), with systematically reduced production costs distributed over millions of chairs. A decisive factor was Thonet's rationalization of the overall logistics—with its own beechwood forests, with factories and worker housing estates constructed near the forests from the company's private supply of stone, with the publication of multilingual sales catalogues

for a continually expanding range of products, with the shipping of the chairs in component parts, and with sales offices in metropolitan business centres around the world. With these practices, established back in the nineteenth century, the company anticipated the strategies of today's market leader IKEA. Both enterprises share the goal of saving costs and both have furnished interiors for generations with their products. While Thonet's abstractions of Biedermeier designs provided streamlined easy-to-use mass furnishing, IKEA's simple forms and colours embody a typically Scandinavian image of solidity and neutrality, which is able to flexibly accommodate varying preferences around the globe.

The difficulty of achieving economy in industrial design is reflected not least in the fact that the costs of developing

strialisierung mit der Imitation des Handwerks anfing und heute in einer Persiflage des Industrieprodukts endet.

EINHEIT

Historisch betrachtet entstanden die Vorzüge des rationalen Industriedesigns in einem dynamischen Prozess, in dem sich neue Technologien und gestalterische Ansätze wechselseitig beeinflussten und in dem die Materialien eine besondere Rolle spielten. Nachdem im 18. Jahrhundert der Eisenguss durch die Verwendung von Gussformen die serielle Herstellung uniformer Stücke rationalisiert hatte, waren es im 19. und frühen 20. Jahrhundert vor allem die Techniken des Biegens von Hölzern und Blechen, die mit wenig Aufwand Formteile aus einem Stück hervorbrachten. Heute entstehen aus gegossenen, gespritzten oder geschäumten Kunststoffen, die noch freier formbar sind und eine einheitliche Färbung sowie homogene Oberflächen erlauben, weit komplexere Formen – bis hin zum kompletten Gegenstand aus einem Material und in einem Arbeitsgang. Dabei führt der Wegfall jeglicher Handarbeit in der Produktion nicht automatisch auch zu ausdruckslosen Produkten, selbst wenn der „Monoblock"-Stuhl als weltweit meistverkaufter Möbeltyp eher ein Beispiel dafür ist, dass Einfachheit nicht nur billig sein, sondern auch billig aussehen kann. In dem Moment, da der Designer letzte Hand an den Prototypen legt, erhält das Produkt sein endgültiges Gesicht, die Perfektion der anschließenden Realisierung aber birgt auch die Gefahr einer Anonymisierung des Entwurfs. Somit besteht die Kunst bei dieser maschinellen Vereinigung von Material, Technik und Form darin, ihr das Hermetische zu nehmen und den Objekten eine Identität zu geben, die sich nicht erst aus dem Vergleich mit Konkurrenzprodukten ergibt, sondern aus ihrer Entstehung ebenso wie aus der Beziehung zwischen Objekt und Benutzer.

Da grundsätzlich gilt, dass die Entwicklung eines Produkts aus einer einzigen Fläche, einer Form oder einem Material die Ressourcen schont und weniger Abfall verursacht, scheint gerade in der Kunststoffverarbeitung die Effizienz durch die Ausnutzung von Substanzen, die erst bei der Herstellung des Produktes entstehen, optimal zu sein. Solche Rechnungen gehen jedoch nur bedingt auf, sofern man die Begrenztheit der Grundstoffe zur Gewinnung der Kunststoffkomponenten und die Ökobilanz am Ende der Lebensdauer eines solchen Fabrikats mit einkalkuliert. Die Verwendung nachwachsender, möglichst lokaler Rohstoffe sowie ein energie- und emissionsarmes Recycling spielen darum eine immer wichtigere Rolle im Design.

INSPIRATION

Wenn sich die Kunst der Reduktion im Design zuletzt in der Art zeigt, wie ein Objekt wieder verschwindet, so zeigt sie sich zuerst in der Art, wie der Entwurf entsteht. Zwei konträre Modelle beziehungsweise unterschiedliche Designertypen stehen hier für die Bandbreite möglicher Ansätze: diejenigen, die sich auf der Suche

----

a product and acquiring the tools of fabrication only become amortized over the course of sales. The "Thonet principle" requires vast production volumes before it begins to pay off. Yet when parameters change, when patents expire and new technologies and competitors enter the market or an economic crisis cripples purchasing power, profitability changes as well. The esteemed glass manufacturer Iittala, for instance, achieved renown in the 1930s with Aino Aalto's designs but found itself in the mid-1990s with an overinflated product range of some 15,000 models. It has now dwindled to a healthy 3,000 designs while still managing to achieve significant increases in turnover. And whereas designers used to gain most of their income from royalties derived from mass-produced articles, nowadays they often earn more from handbuilt prototypes that do not involve any follow-up production. Thus, we are brought full circle: what began, at the start of industrialization, with the imitation of handicraft has ended up today as a parody of industrial products.

UNITY

Historically, the advantages of rational industrial design have emerged from a dynamic process in which new technologies and design approaches influenced one another, with materials playing a prominent role in the interaction. After iron casting streamlined the serial manufacture of uniform components in the eighteenth century (through the use of casting moulds), the nineteenth and early twentieth centuries saw the greatest advances in creating shaped parts from one piece of material, through the techniques of wood bending and metal sheeting. Today far more complex forms are produced using cast, sprayed, and foamed plastics, which are even more freely formable and allow uniform dyeing as well as homogeneous surfaces, and sometimes even yielding complete objects from a single piece of material in just one step. The absence of the human touch in such fabrication processes does not automatically lead to expressionless products, even if the worldwide top-selling "monobloc" chair makes the case that simplicity can mean a cheap look in addition to cheap costs. After the designer puts the finishing touches on the prototype, the product is given its final countenance, yet the perfection of the subsequent realization process also carries the risk of producing an anonymous design. With such machine-driven unification of material, technology, and form, the trick is to suppress the hermetic qualities and give objects an identity that does not merely result from comparisons with competing products but from the process of creation as well as from the relationship between object and user.

In light of the general rule that

nach Perfektion an einer vorgegebenen oder selbst geschriebenen Geschichte von Vorbildern abarbeiten, und diejenigen, die wie Pablo Picasso sagen würden: „Ich suche nicht, ich finde!" – kurz: der „Sklave" und das „Genie". Damit sei jedoch keineswegs gesagt, dass Letztere auch die größere Leistung vollbringen, denn tatsächlich stehen die „Genies" unter den Designern nicht unbedingt für nachhaltiges Design. Ihre Entwürfe sind Einfälle, die den Nagel des Zeitgeists zwar auf den Kopf treffen mögen, denen aber genau deshalb für den dauerhaften Erfolg die Zeitlosigkeit fehlt. Luigi Colani, Philippe Starck und Ron Arad haben zwar auch „Klassik-verdächtige" Objekte entworfen, aber im Grunde sind sie Helden des Moments, während Michael Thonet, Charles und Ray Eames oder Jasper Morrison als Langzeitsieger dastehen.

Der Unterschied liegt, bei aller nötigen Generalisierung, tatsächlich in der Arbeitsweise. Während die „Genies" Formen erfinden, deren Prägnanz eine kurze, aber heftige Aufmerksamkeit am Markt erzielt, limitieren die „Sklaven" ihr kreatives Ego und kommen erst durch systematisches Durchspielen von Varianten in einem oft auch für den Hersteller aufwändigen Prozess zu ausgereiften Lösungen. Während Ludwig Mies van der Rohe also auf den „Gott im Detail" als Vollkommenheit im Kleinsten verwies und seine Vorbilder genau studierte, um zu aufgeräumten, klareren Strukturen zu fin-

den, erscheint die Kunst der Reduktion in den aus *objets trouvés* zusammengesetzten Entwürfen eines Tejo Remy wie eine Abkürzung dieses Verfahrens und liest sich eher als ästhetisches Statement oder Gebrauchsanleitung zur Eigeninitiative, denn als alltagstaugliches Design. So wie diese Genialität jedoch riskiert, als Eintagsfliege zu verenden, so ist allerdings auch die Perfektionierung nicht davor gefeit, von äußeren Entwicklungen überrannt zu werden oder sich schon im Entwurfsstadium totzulaufen. Ludwig Wittgenstein beispielsweise zeichnete für die Villa seiner Schwester „jedes Fenster, jede Tür, jeden Riegel der Fenster, jeden Heizkörper mit einer Genauigkeit, als wären es Präzisionsinstrumente"[11], bedauerte aber später seinen Anteil am asketischen Formalismus des Hauses: „[…] das ursprüngliche Leben, das wilde Leben, welches sich austoben möchte – fehlt. Man könnte also auch sagen, es fehlt ihm die Gesundheit."[12]

FUNKTIONALITÄT, VERDICHTUNG, LEICHTIGKEIT
George Nelsons Hinweis „Die besten Formen, die die Menschen hervorbringen, sind die, bei denen es ums Überleben geht, denn Fragen von Tod und Leben spornen nun einmal stärker an als Fragen des Marketings."[13] meint jedoch genau diese, auf ihre nackten Funktionen reduzierten Werkzeuge, bei denen jedes überflüssige Detail gefährlich werden

Ludwig Wittgenstein / Peter Engelmann, *Haus Wittgenstein* (gebaut für Margarethe Stonborough-Wittgenstein), Wien 1926–1928, Fotografie aus dem Taschenfotobuch von Ludwig Wittgenstein, The Cambridge Wittgenstein Archive.

Ludwig Wittgenstein / Peter Engelmann, *Wittgenstein House* (built for Margarethe Stonborough-Wittgenstein), Vienna 1926–1928, photograph from the pocket photo book of Ludwig Wittgenstein, The Cambridge Wittgenstein Archive.

products developed from a single plane, form, or material save resources and yield less waste, plastics processing seems to offer optimal efficiency in utilizing substances created simultaneously with the fabrication of the product. Such advantages do not necessarily pan out, however, when one factors in the scarcity of the raw materials used to create the plastic components and the ecological balance sheet at the end of the product's service life. For this reason, the use of renewable, locally sourced raw materials and low-energy, low-emission recycling plays an increasingly important role in design.

INSPIRATION
If the art of reduction in design is ultimately shown in the way an object makes its final disappearance, it is initially demonstrated by the manner in which the design first emerges. Two

contrasting models or designer typologies demarcate the spectrum of possible approaches: those who labour on a given or self-scripted history of precursory models in search of perfection and those who, as Pablo Picasso would say, "don't seek, but find!" In short, the "slave" and the "genius". This, however, does not mean that the latter renders the greater service, for the "geniuses" among designers do not necessarily stand for sustainable design. While their bold inspirations may hit squarely upon the zeitgeist, precisely for this reason they lack the timelessness necessary for lasting success. Luigi Colani, Philippe Starck, and Ron Arad have designed objects seemingly destined to go down in history as classics, but in general they are heroes of the moment, while Michael Thonet, Charles and Ray Eames, and

Jasper Morrison stay the course as longterm winners.

Generalizing for the sake of discussion, the difference lies in their work methods. While the "geniuses" invent forms whose captivating novelty generates brief but intense market hype, the "slaves" keep their creative ego in check and arrive at fully developed solutions by systematically playing through possible variants in a process that is often lengthy for both the designer and manufacturer. While Ludwig Mies van der Rohe referred to perfection on the micro-level as "the God in the details" and studied preceding models to find clearer, more orderly structures, the art of reduction exhibited by the designs of Tejo Remy, put together from *objets trouvés*, appears to shortcut this process and can be read more as an aesthetic statement or instructive lesson in entrepreneurial initiative than as design suited for

kann. Die konsequenteste Minimierung von Materialverbrauch, Volumen und Gewicht und die einfachste Handhabung finden wir deshalb auch dort, wo die Bedingungen am härtesten sind: beim Militär, im Sport und im Verkehr.

„Bauen Sie ein Auto, das Platz für zwei Bauern in Stiefeln und einen Zentner Kartoffeln oder ein Fässchen Wein bietet, einen Schirm auf vier Rädern"[14], so lauteten die Instruktionen Citroëns an den Konstrukteur André Lefèbvre, mit denen er 1934 aufgefordert wurde, einen Kleinstwagen, den späteren 2CV, zu entwickeln. Außerdem sollte das Auto „so viel wie möglich Komfort" bieten, „eine Spitzengeschwindigkeit von 60 kmh, einen Benzinverbrauch von 3 l auf 100 km und ein Gewicht von 300 kg, und das alles zu einem Drittel des Preises des 7CV *Traction Avant*."[15]

Mit dem Projekt einer *voiture maximum* verfolgte Le Corbusier dieses Ziel schon 1928. Schließlich wollte der Schweizer Architekt, der auch seine Utopie einer neuen Stadt für drei Millionen Einwohner ohne rigoros minimierte Strukturen schlicht nicht hätte formulieren können, Citroën dazu bewegen, in den Baumarkt einzusteigen.[16]

Nach dem Automobil bedeutete die Überwindung der Schwerkraft durch die Fliegerei die zweite große Inspiration, welche Architekten, Künstler und Designer zu Experimenten mit leichteren Materialien und luftigeren Formen beflügelte. Dem Vorbild der Flugmaschinen sollten zu Beginn des 20. Jahrhunderts auch am Boden neue Apparate für ein befreites, unbeschwertes Leben folgen, denn die rasante Zunahme von Bevölkerungswachstum, Mobilität und Kommunikation verdichtete den Alltag in Bezug auf Raum und Zeit – eine Entwicklung, die bis in die digitale und virtuelle Welt von heute reicht. Als immer mehr Büros in innerstädtische Hochhäuser drängten, die sich nur noch über die Kleinsträume der elektrischen Aufzüge erschließen ließen, begann man auch im sozialen Wohnungsbau nach Platz sparenden Alternativen zu suchen. Vor allem deutsche Architekten und Designer ließen sich damals von amerikanischen Fabriken inspirieren, die nach den wissenschaftlichen Methoden des Ökonomen Frederic Winslow Taylor und des Auto-Produzenten Henry Ford funktionierten. Mitte der 1920er Jahre förderten die deutschen Sozialdemokraten einen von der Bauhaus-Architektur beeinflussten sozialen Wohnungsbau, dessen nach rationalen Prinzipien konzipierte, gebaute und funktionierende „Maschinen-Architektur" sich aus dem Glauben an eine mechanisierte Welt speiste.[17] Den Bauten entsprach die Möblierung: Neben vielen anderen Lösungen aus falt- und stapelbaren Einrichtungen gehörten Grete Schütte-Lihotzkys Platz und Zeit sparend gestaltete *Frankfurter Küche* und Ferdinand Kramers Typenmöbel aus genormten, modularen, also billigen, mobilen und vielseitigen Elementen, die aus Untersuchungen zur effizienten Wohnraumnutzung hervorgegangen waren, zu den erfolgreichsten Resultaten dieser Entwicklung.

----

everyday use. Yet as such bold ingenuity risks becoming a flash in the pan, the slow-going, perfection-oriented approach is not immune to being overrun by external developments or fizzling out already in the design phase. In the villa of his sister, for instance, Ludwig Wittgenstein "designed every window and door, every window lock and radiator, with as much care and attention to detail as if they were precision instruments",[11] yet later regretted the ascetic formalism of the house: "primordial life, wild life striving to erupt into the open—that is lacking. And so you might say, health is lacking."[12]

FUNCTIONALITY, COMPACTION, AND LIGHTNESS
George Nelson's remark that "[t]he best man-made designs are survival designs, simply because they deal with life and death rather than marketing considerations"[13] refers precisely to those tools reduced to their bare functions in which each superfluous detail can even be dangerous. The most stringent minimization of material, volume, and weight and the simplest handling can therefore be found where conditions are the hardest: in the military, in sports, and in transportation.

"Build a car for two farmers dressed for work, carrying along either 50 kilos of potatoes or a small barrel of wine, an umbrella on four wheels."[14] Such were the reputed instructions in Citroën's 1934 briefing to engineer André Lefèbvre for the development of a mini-car, which would later become the 2CV. Further requirements were for "maximum comfort, a top speed of 60kph, a fuel consumption of three litres per 100 kilometres and a weight of 300 kilograms, all for one third of the retail price of the 7CV Traction Avant".[15] With the project of a *voiture maximum*, Le Corbusier had pursued this same concept back in 1928. After all, the Swiss-born architect, whose plans for a new utopian city for three million inhabitants would have been simply impossible without rigorously minimized structures, sought to encourage Citroën to enter the construction market.[16]

Along with the automobile, the defiance of gravity through aviation provided architects, artists, and designers with a second major source of inspiration, spurring them to experiment with lighter materials and airier forms. At the beginning of the twentieth century, the model of flying machines was emulated on the ground with new devices for a liberated, light-spirited way of living, oriented to address the rapid increase in population, mobility, and communication that had brought about a densification of daily life with respect to space and time—a development that reaches into today's digital and virtual world. As more and more offices

GEOMETRIE

Ein Konzentrat der praktischen und ästhetischen Überlegungen zur minimalistischen Architektur stellten damals das 1923 am Weimarer Bauhaus konzipierte *Haus am Horn* und Gerrit Thomas Rietvelds im Jahr darauf in Utrecht gebautes *Haus Schröder* dar. Während man in Weimar, um die Grundbedürfnisse einer kleinen Familie mit bescheidenen Mitteln zu decken, über einem quadratischen, eingeschossigen Grundriss das zentrale Wohnzimmer in einen Rahmen aus Schlaf- und Funktionsräumen fasste, löste Rietveld die Aufgabe mit einem zweigeschossigen Kubus, den er wie ein kompliziertes Kastenmöbel verschachtelte, das sich über die Verstellbarkeit seiner Bestandteile erschließt. Und während sich das *Haus am Horn*, wiewohl für eventuelle Anbauten angelegt, als weißer Baukörper aus standardisierten Teilen hermetisch präsentiert, öffnet sich das *Haus Schröder* durch Schiebewände und eine großzügige Verglasung ins Innere und nach außen. Seine asymmetrische Komposition aus gleichsam aneinander vorbeigleitenden, rechteckigen Volumen in Weiß, Schwarz und den Grundfarben scheint den Bau seiner Masse und seines Gewichts und damit auch, der möglichst vielseitigen Nutzung entsprechend, einer festen Orientierung zu entheben.

„Man hat […] versucht, alle Teile in ihrer Einzigartigkeit zu belassen, und zwar in der jeweils ursprünglichen Form nach Art des Gebrauchs und Materials, der Form, die am besten geeignet ist, in Proportion zu den anderen Teilen eine Harmonie zu erzielen. Die konstruktive Form trägt dazu bei, dass die Teile unverändert miteinander verbunden werden, so dass der eine Teil den anderen möglichst wenig dominiert oder selbst als untergeordnet erscheint, damit das Ganze vor allem frei und klar im Raum steht und die Form das Material beherrscht."[18] Mit dieser Beschreibung, nicht vom *Haus Schröder*, sondern von Rietvelds *Roodblauwe Stoel* von 1918, formulierte Rietveld zugleich Prinzipien der De Stijl-Gruppe, die für das Design am Bauhaus, vor allem seit Theo van Doesburgs Weimarer Vorträgen im Jahr 1922, von großem Einfluss waren. Das grundlegende Motiv, welches das Bauhaus wie auch De Stijl bestimmte, war dabei eine Geometrie, die einerseits der idealisierten Industrieproduktion entsprach und andererseits durch die Ausstrahlung afrikanischer Skulptur und japanischer Baukunst geprägt war. Ohne den Kubismus, der seine Figuren expressiv aus autonomen geometrischen Formen zusammensetzte, wären De Stijl und der russische Konstruktivismus so undenkbar wie die am Bauhaus ebenfalls beachteten Readymades Marcel Duchamps. Und ohne den Import japanischer Kultur, der all diesen künstlerischen Revolutionen um Jahre vorausging und auf zahlreiche Gestalter wie eine Erweckung gewirkt hatte, hätten sich damals wohl auch in Europa die Wände nicht verschoben.

Nachdem sich Japan mehr als 200 Jahre von der Außenwelt abgeschottet hatte, muss das Land nach seiner Öffnung in den 1850er Jahren dem industrialisierten Westen beinahe als außerir-

----

crowded into inner-city high-rises only accessible through the compact spaces of electric lifts, designers and planners began looking for space-saving alternatives in social housing as well. In particular, German architects and designers of the era took inspiration from American factories, which operated according to the scientific methods of the economist Frederic Winslow Taylor and the automaker Henry Ford. In the mid-1920s, the German Social Democrats called for housing influenced by Bauhaus architecture, whose "machine architecture" was conceived, built, and utilized according to rational principles rooted in the belief in a mechanized world.[17] The buildings were matched by corresponding furniture, and among the many foldable and stackable furnishing solutions, the most successful results of this development included Grete Schütte-Lihotzky's space- and time-saving *Frankfurter Küche* and Ferdinand Kramer's Typenmöbel, which were made from standardized, modular, and hence inexpensive mobile and versatile elements, based on investigations into the efficient use of the living space.

GEOMETRY

That same decade, a concentration of practical and aesthetic considerations concerning minimalistic architecture was to be found in the *Haus am Horn*, conceived at the Weimar Bauhaus in 1923, and in Gerrit Thomas Rietveld's *Schröder House*, built the following year in Utrecht. Seeking to cover basic needs for a small family of modest means, those in Weimar devised a quadratic, one-story floor plan with a central living space framed by bedrooms and other auxiliary units. For his part, Rietveld solved the task at hand with a two-storey cube nested like an intricate piece of case furniture, made accessible through the adjustability of its components. And while the *Haus am Horn*, despite being designed to accommodate potential future additions, appeared as a hermetic white volume of standardized parts, the *Schröder House* opened up internally and externally through sliding panels and expansive glazing. Arranged in an asymmetrical composition, the rectangular volumes in white, black, and primary colours seem to slip and slide past one another, divesting the building of mass and weight and, hence, of a fixed orientation in order to allow for the widest possible range of uses.

"[A]n attempt has been made to have every part simple and in its most elementary form in accordance with function and material, the form, thus, which is most capable of being harmonized with the whole. The construction is attuned to the parts to ensure that no part dominates or is subordinate to the others. In this way, the whole stands freely and clearly in space, and the form

dische Zivilisation erschienen sein, zumindest als Gegenentwurf der eigenen Lebenswelt in Form eines hoch gezüchteten, kuriosen Gesamtkunstwerks: von der Kunst des Blumenarrangements, den Bonsai oder der Teezeremonie bis hin zu fremdartigen Gegenständen sowie Menschen, die den größten Wert auf Reinlichkeit legen und sich in weitgehend leeren Räumen bewegen. Für die Verbreitung dieses durchaus realistischen Japan-Bildes sorgten, damals neben bedeutenden Ausstellungen vor allem *Ukiyo-e*-Holzschnitte mit Darstellungen des Alltags, die in Japan so populär waren wie heute das Fernsehprogramm. In scharf umrissenen, schattenlosen Figuren auf einer zweidimensionalen Bildebene mit unmodellierten Farbflächen vermittelten sie dem Westen nicht nur eine neue Bildsprache, sondern die lebhafte Ansicht einer Kultur, deren Formulierungen immer noch Funktionen – und seien sie ästhetischer Natur – zuzuschreiben waren. Zudem weckten sie die Sehnsucht nach einer lebendigen Einheit des Menschen mit seiner Umwelt und regten dadurch vielfach zur programmatischen Zusammenarbeit von Technik und Künsten an.[19]

Als Frank Lloyd Wright 1910 und 1911 im Berliner Wasmuth Verlag sein damals schon so innovatives wie umfangreiches Werk veröffentlichte, demonstrierte er den Europäern

nicht die Kompetenz für die technischen Möglichkeiten der Hochhausarchitektur, die er in Chicago erworben hatte, er zeigte nicht einmal Fotografien seiner „ausgeführten Bauten und Entwürfe". Stattdessen überraschte er mit losen Blättern von Außen- und Innenansichten einer Architektur, deren Adaption von Merkmalen der japanischen Baukunst den Raumplan westlicher Architektur aus den Angeln hob. Wrights Faszination für Japans Kultur, die mit der Besichtigung eines Pavillons auf der Chicagoer Weltausstellung 1893 begann, führte 1905 zu seiner ersten Japanreise, von der er als Sammler von *Ukiyo-e*-Drucken heimkehrte, die er später seinen Bauherren auch verkaufte. Die in Helldunkelkontrasten orthogonal gerahmten japanischen Bauten aus einfachen Holzstützen und -balken ohne tragende Wände und mit weit vorstehenden Dächern, einer variablen Gliederung der Wohnfläche nach dem menschlichen, aber standardisierten Maß der *Tatami*-Matte sowie großzügigen Öffnungen zwischen den Räumen und in die Umgebung waren eine Offenbarung für den Architekten, der seit seiner Kindheit auf der Suche nach geometrischen Prinzipien der Natur war.[20]

Die von Wright entworfenen Räume, die unter den abgeflachten Dächern seiner Häuser zwischen zurücktretenden, durchbrochenen oder beiseite geschobenen Wänden inein-

Marcel Duchamp, *Roue de bicyclette* (Fahrrad-Rad), 1951 (Replik nach dem verschollenen Original aus dem Jahr 1913), Assemblage: Metallrad auf bemaltem Holzhocker, 128,3 x 63,8 x 42 cm, The Sidney and Harriet Janis Collection, The Museum of Modern Art, New York/Scala, Florence.

Marcel Duchamp, *Roue de bicyclette* (Bicycle Wheel), 1951 (Reconstruction after the lost original of 1913), Assemblage: metal wheel, mounted on painted wood stool, 128.3 x 63.8 x 42 cm. The Sidney and Harriet Janis Collection, The Museum of Modern Art, New York / Scala, Florence.

stands out from the material."[18] With this description, not of *Schröder House* but of his *Roodblauwe Stoel* from 1918, Rietveld articulated the principles of the De Stijl group, which had influenced the Bauhaus, especially in the area of design, since the Weimar lectures given by Theo van Doesburg in 1922. Yet the core motif that defined both the Bauhaus and De Stijl was geometry— on one hand, conforming to the ideal of industrial production and, on the other, endorsing the influence of African sculpture and Japanese architecture. Without Cubism's expressive compositions of autonomous geometric forms, De Stijl and Russian Constructivism would have been just as inconceivable as the readymades of Marcel Duchamp, which likewise attracted considerable interest at the Bauhaus. And without the import of Japanese culture that preceded all these

artistic revolutions by many years and acted as an awakening for numerous designers, the walls would never have shifted in twentieth-century Europe either.

After Japan reopened its gates in 1850, following over two centuries of self-imposed isolation from the outside world, the country must have appeared to the industrialized West as an almost extraterrestrial civilization or, at least, as a distinct counter-scheme to its own way of life, bearing the form of a highly cultivated and curious *gesamtkunstwerk*: from the art of flower arranging through bonsai and tea ceremony traditions to

the unfamiliar objects employed by a nation that attached utmost importance to cleanliness and to living in largely empty interiors. Along with a number of significant exhibitions, a key role in disseminating this quite realistic picture of Japan was played by *ukiyo-e* woodblock prints, which depicted daily life and were as popular in Japan as today's television programmes. In sharply delineated, shadowless figures on a two-dimensional image plane with flat, unmodelled areas of colour, they not only offered the West a new pictorial language but also a lively view of a culture whose formulations could still be attributed to functions—including those of an aesthetic nature. Moreover, they aroused the longing for a vital unity of man with his environment, in many cases inspiring programmatic collaboration between technology and the arts.[19]

ander fließen und die er bis ins Detail aufgelöst in den Konturen geometrischer Volumen zeigte,[21] fanden vor allem in Holland und Deutschland einflussreiche Bewunderer. Nicht nur Peter Behrens, der sich Blätter aus der Wasmuth-Mappe ins Büro hing, und sein Schüler Mies van der Rohe, der sie dort sah, studierten die Entwürfe eingehend,[22] sondern wohl auch Gerrit Rietveld. Wrights Zeichnungen des nach den Prinzipien seiner Bauten konstruierten Mobiliars[23] zeigen sich nämlich als direkte Vorläufer der frühen Möbel Rietvelds – besonders des *Roodblauwe Stoel*, dessen erste, unbemalte Fassung von van Doesburg zum Modell für die „(abstrakt-realistischen) Skulpturen in unserem zukünftigen Interieur"[24] erklärt wurde.

Auch Le Corbusier sah die Architektur als eine Domäne der Kunst, doch im Gegensatz zu Wright, De Stijl und dem Bauhaus war sie für ihn eine „reine Schöpfung des Geistes"[25]. So komponierte er puristische Räume aus Kuben, Kegeln, Zylindern und Pyramiden, die millimetergenau stimmen mussten, um dem Wesen der modernen Technologie und dem Ausdruck „zeitloser ästhetischer Gesetze"[26] zu entsprechen. Während aber Le Corbusier bei Klosterzellen wie bei Sozialwohnungen immer noch einen menschlichen Maßstab anlegte und sein Mobiliar – übrigens in Übereinstimmung mit den Auffassungen Adolf Loos'[27] – als ein im Wesentlichen historisch geronnenes „Konzentrat von Formen, die geeignet sind, sich mit dem Körper zu harmonisieren",[28] verstand, erstarrte die Geometrie im perfektionistischen Minimalismus zahlloser Postmoderner, die in das Vakuum ihrer Räume Badewannen mit den ergonomischen Qualitäten von Soldatensärgen stellen, zu einem schlicht unpraktischen Funktionalismus.

ABSTRAKTION

Einrichtungen, mit denen wir in engen Körperkontakt kommen, empfinden wir als angenehm, wenn sie aus natürlichen, lebendigen Materialien bestehen und anatomisch geformt sind. Thonets Beispiel zeigte, wie eine dem Verhalten der Naturmaterialien wie auch dem menschlichen Körper entsprechende Gestalt nicht nur auf die praktischen Anforderungen reduziert, sondern auch ökonomisch hergestellt werden kann. Ihm folgte 1927 Rietveld, der – von der Linienführung des Stahlrohrs in den Bauhausmöbeln Marcel Breuers beeindruckt – Sitz und Rücken eines Stuhls aus einem durchgehenden Sperrholz bog.[29] Wenig später entwickelte der Finne Alvar Aalto aus gebogenem Sperrholz auch die tragenden Gestelle für solch geschwungene Flächen. Den ökonomischen Durchbruch organischer Abstraktion schafften aber erst nach dem Zweiten Weltkrieg Charles und Ray Eames, wobei Rays Beitrag zu dieser Entwicklung sicher nicht nur im Gespür für Form- und Farbgebung lag, sondern auch in der Kraft der plastischen Abstraktion.[30] Fünf Jahre nachdem Charles Eames mit Eero Saarinen unter großem Aufwand Sperrholzlagen zu verschiedenen Arten von Sitz-Rückenschalen verformt hatte, fanden er und seine Frau Ray 1945 zurück zu einer Trennung von Sitz

----

When Frank Lloyd Wright published his strikingly innovative and comprehensive portfolio with Ernst Wasmuth in Berlin in 1910 and 1911, he did not demonstrate to Europeans the technical competence he had acquired from high-rise architecture in Chicago, nor did he choose to present photographic documentation of his "Executed Buildings and Designs". Instead, he took readers by surprise with unbound lithographs showing exterior and interior drawings of an architectural style whose adaption of the Japanese building aesthetic unhinged the spatial planning of Western architecture. Initially sparked by a visit to a pavilion at the 1893 Chicago World's Fair, Wright's fascination with Japanese culture led to his first trip to the country in 1905, returning as an avid collector of *ukiyo-e* prints that he later even sold to select clients. Orthogonally framed in contrasts of light and dark, the Japanese structures— built with simple wooden supports and beams, lacking load-bearing walls, and employing wide projecting roofs, a variable disposition of the living space (according to the standardized yet human scale of the *tatami* mat), and expansive openings between the rooms and out into the surroundings—were a revelation for the architect, who had been drawn to the geometric principles of nature since childhood.[20]

Flowing into one another beneath flattened roofs, through non-continuous and receding or shifting walls and partitions, and articulated down to the smallest detail in the contours of geometric volumes,[21] Wright's interior schemes attracted influential admirers, especially in Germany and the Netherlands. The designs were studied in-depth not only by Peter Behrens, who hung sheets from the Wasmuth portfolio in his office where they were likewise encountered and absorbed by his student Mies van der Rohe,[22] but presumably also by Gerrit Rietveld. Wright's drawings of furnishings constructed according to the same principles as his buildings[23] show themselves to be direct predecessors of early furniture by Rietveld—especially the *Roodblauwe Stoel*, whose initial uncoloured version was declared by van Doesburg to be a model for the "(abstract-real) images of our future interior".[24]

Le Corbusier also saw architecture as a domain of art, though for him, in contrast to Wright, De Stijl, and the Bauhaus, it was a "pure creation of the mind".[25] He thus composed puristic spaces from cubes, cones, cylinders, and pyramids, measured down to the exact millimetre, in keeping with the essence of modern technology and as an expression of "timeless aesthetic laws".[26] Yet while Le Corbusier still applied a human scale, from monastery cells to social housing units, and understood his furni-

und Rücken aus Sperrholz, die sie unabhängig voneinander ergonomisch verformten und über Gummistücke in einem Gestell verbanden und so in den Raum stellten, dass sie sich dem Körper optimal anschmiegten. Über Versuche mit Metallblech gelangten sie Anfang der 1950er Jahre dann mit einer Sitz-Rückenschale aus Fiberglas zur ökonomischen und formalen Minimallösung.

In der Architektur hatte das von natürlichen Formentwicklungen hergeleitete Design seine Entsprechung in einem bionisch inspirierten Schmelzprozess quasi zurück zum Ei, der um die Jahrhundertwende die Bauten Victor Hortas in Brüssel und Antoni Gaudís in Barcelona erfasste und sich später in den anthroposophischen Gebäuden um Rudolf Steiners *Goetheanum* in Dornach fortsetzte. Ab Mitte der 1920er Jahre entwickelte auch Friedrich Kiesler, der mit Constantin Brâncusi gut bekannt war,[31] Konzepte für ein organisches Raumkontinuum, die über nicht realisierte Entwürfe seiner *Space-* und *Endless-Houses* schließlich im Jerusalemer Museum *Schrein des Buches* von 1965 gipfelten, mit dem er eine Steilvorlage für Matti Suuronens *Futuro-Haus* aus Kunststoff von 1968 lieferte, das in der schon von Kiesler formulierten Idealform der liegenden Ellipse auch seriell hergestellt werden konnte.[32]

Bezeichnenderweise hatte Lehm, als einer der ältesten Baustoffe der Menschheit, an dieser Entwicklung keinerlei Anteil, obwohl er sich mit geringstem Aufwand

bereitstellen, frei verformen und ohne Rückstände entsorgen oder wieder verwenden lässt. Ein Grund dafür liegt wohl darin, dass er von jeder Generation erneuert werden muss, wobei in genau solcher Beschäftigung mit der eigenen Umwelt ein Schlüssel zu jener Einheit läge, die wir eingangs für die Shaker beschrieben haben. Dass aber auch kein anderer der genannten Ansätze das Bauwesen grundlegend veränderte, mag ein Indiz für unsere Gewöhnung an ein rechtwinkliges Koordinatensystem sein, welches das Chaos der Welt für uns ordnet. Kiesler erwies sich mit seinem Konzept zumindest im Design als ein Pionier organisch abstrakter Formgebung, als er in New York um 1937 einander ergänzende Couchtische entwarf, die die Nierentische der 1950er Jahre vorwegnahmen, und 1942 für Peggy Guggenheims Galerie „Art of This Century" ein sphärisch gekrümmtes Interieur mit Möbeln schuf, die den Amöben aus den Reliefs Hans Arps ähnlich sehen und deren freie Form eine freie Nutzung als Schaukelstühle für die Besucher ebenso ermöglichte wie als Podeste für die Kunst.

AUFLÖSUNG UND TRANSPARENZ
Wenn es dem Einfluss von Designern wie Rietveld, Breuer, Aalto oder Kiesler, Saarinen und den Eames' zu verdanken ist, dass das Mobiliar moderner Haushalte insgesamt „‚sauberer' in der Linie und leichter in der Masse"[33] wurde, so ist

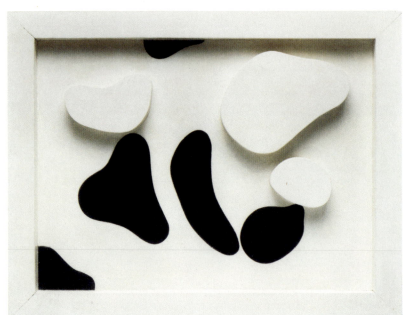

Hans Arp, Relief: *Constellation selon les lois du hasard* (Konstellation nach den Gesetzen des Zufalls), um 1930, Holz bemalt, 54,9 x 69,8 cm, Tate, London, Hinterlassenschaft E.C. Gregory 1959.

Hans Arp, Relief: *Constellation selon les lois du hasard* (Constellation According to the Laws of Chance), c. 1930, painted wood, 54.9 x 69.8 cm, Tate, London, bequeathed by E.C. Gregory 1959.

ture—incidentally, akin to the views of Adolf Loos[27]—as a historically coagulated "concentration of forms suited to harmonization with the body,"[28] geometry became hardened into plainly impractical functionalism in the perfectionistic minimalism of countless postmodernists, outfitting their vacuum-like interiors with bathtubs as ergonomic as a soldier's coffin.

ABSTRACTION
Furnishings that we come into close physical contact with are viewed as satisfying and pleasant when made of natural, lively materials with anatomically fitted contours. Thonet's example showed how a form accommodating the characteristics of both natural materials and the human body could not only be reduced to practical requirements but also be produced in accordance with economic principles. In 1927, this model was followed by Rietveld who—impressed by the lines of the Bauhaus tubular steel furniture designed by Marcel Breuer—bent the seat and back of a chair out of one continuous piece of plywood.[29] Shortly thereafter, the Finn Alvar Aalto developed bases out of bent plywood to support such curving surfaces. The economic breakthrough in organic abstraction did not arrive, however, until after the Second World War with the designs of Charles and Ray Eames, whereby Ray's contribution to this development certainly lay not only in the feeling for shape and colour but also in the power of plastic abstraction.[30] Five years after Charles Eames had teamed up with Eero Saarinen in an exhaustive effort to mould plywood layers into various one-piece seat shells, he and his wife Ray returned in 1945 to the idea of separate seat and back elements made of plywood, with each piece ergonomically moulded and connected to the frame with pieces of rubber and thus positioned in space to allow optimal adaption to the body. Through experimentations with sheet metal, the couple hit in the early 1950s upon the economically and formally successful minimalist solution of a one-piece seat shell made of fibreglass.

Design derived from natural forms had its architectural equivalent in a bionically inspired melding process leading back to the metaphorical egg, represented by the turn-of-the-century structures of Victor Horta in Brussels and Antoni Gaudí in Barcelona and later continued in the anthroposophical buildings of Rudolf Steiner's *Goetheanum* in Dornach. Beginning in the mid-1920s, concepts for an organic continuum of space were being developed by Friedrich Kiesler, who

die Radikalität ihrer Lösungen technischen Errungenschaften ebenso zu verdanken wie einem Dialog mit der sich rasant zwischen abstrakt, konkret, surrealistisch oder konzeptionell verändernden Kunst, der sich nach dem Zweiten Weltkrieg intensivierte und immer wieder Grenzlinien der Disziplinen infrage stellt. Dass dabei auch die Kunst auf wissenschaftliche und technische Neuerungen reagierte, welche das Weltbild wandelten, versteht sich von selbst.

Das Aufheben von unverrückbar geglaubten Grundfesten, wie es sich schon im Motiv der frei im Raum gleitenden Körper bei Wright, Malewitsch und Rietveld zeigte und ebenso in El Lissitzkys *Proun*-Installationen als „Umsteigestationen zu neuen, als ‚schwebend‘ vorstellbaren Bauten"[34], war stets auch als Anregung gemeint, den Menschen mit fundamentalen Mitteln aus seinen Gebundenheiten zu befreien und in eine neue Balance zu bringen. Entsprechend wurden die Auflösung der Materie, die Schönheit des Lichts, und die Kontrolle über die Energie wiederholt als imposante Monumente für Weltausstellungen inszeniert: in Joseph Paxtons Londoner *Kristallpalast* (1851), dem Pariser *Eiffelturm* (1889), in Mies van der Rohes *Barcelona Pavillon* (1929), dem Brüsseler *Atomium* (1958), in Richard Buckminster Fullers *Geodesic Dome* in Montreal (1967) oder Peter Zumthors *Klangkörper* in Hannover (2000).

Die technischen Möglichkeiten, die Effizienz des Materials auszureizen, als ökonomisches und heute vor allem auch ökologisches Anliegen, wurden im 20. Jahrhundert enorm erweitert beziehungsweise ersetzt durch Möglichkeiten, die Materie intelligent zu überlisten und einen gewünschten Effekt nur noch mit Elektrizität, Wellen und Strahlung zu bewirken. Heute ist das längst eine alltägliche Realität, die Designer und Architekten zwingt, in allen Bereichen immer enger mit den Ingenieuren zusammenzuarbeiten. Eine Revolution bedeutete aber 1925 bereits am Bauhaus Marcel Breuers Einführung des Stahlrohrs in den Haushalt. Walter Gropius' Vorgabe einer „maschinenproduktion als modernstem mittel der gestaltung"[35] folgend und beeindruckt von der Stabilität seines neuen Fahrrads entwarf Breuer mit dem *Wassily* einen bis aufs Gerippe konzentrierten Sessel, den er als letzten Etappensieg einer konsequenten Reduktion des Materials darstellte, bevor es möglich sein sollte, auf „einer elastischen Luftsäule" zu sitzen.[36] Gegenüber Rietvelds *Roodblauwe Stoel* stellte das maschinenartige Gerüst aus spiegelnden, über den Boden gleitenden Rohren sowie Sitz, Rücken- und Armlehnen aus metallisch glänzenden Stoffbändern eine noch fortschrittlichere Entmaterialisierung dar. Nachdem El Lissitzky mit seinem *Wolkenbügel* die kühne Idee eines in luftiger Höhe wie schwerelos auskragenden Gebäudes veröffentlicht hatte,

Bauhaus-Szene: Lis Beyer oder Ise Gropius mit Theatermaske im Stahlrohr-Armlehnsessel von Marcel Breuer von 1925, um 1926, Foto: Erich Consemüller, Bauhaus-Archiv Berlin.

Bauhaus-scene: Lis Beyer or Ise Gropius with a theatre mask by Oskar Schlemmer sitting on Marcel Breuer's tubular steel club armchair executed in 1925, ca. 1926, photograph: Erich Consemüller, courtesy of Bauhaus-Archiv Berlin.

was well acquainted with the elemental forms of Constantin Brâncusi.[31] From the never-realized designs of his *Space House* and *Endless House* up to the 1965 *Shrine of the Book* at the Israel Museum in Jerusalem, Kiesler laid the groundwork for Matti Suuronen's 1968 *Futuro* house in reinforced plastic, which could be mass produced in the ideal form of the horizontal ellipse previously elaborated by Kiesler.[32]

Significantly, clay played no part in this development despite being one of the oldest building materials known to civilization, able to be produced with little effort, shaped freely, disposed of with no residual waste, and even reused again. A likely reason is that this material has to be rediscovered and restored by each generation, even though precisely such an engagement with one's own environment would be key to the earlier-described unity illustrated by

the Shakers. But the fact that none of the hitherto mentioned approaches fundamentally changed the practice of building may be an indication of our well-entrenched adaption to an orthogonal coordinate system, which orders the chaos of the world for us. With his concept of the horizontal ellipse, Kiesler proved to be a pioneer of organically abstracted forms, at least in the field of design, as is attested in the complementary nesting coffee tables he created in New York in the mid-1930s (anticipating the kidney-shaped tables of the 1950s) and later, in 1942, when he devised a spherically curved interior for Peggy Guggenheim's Art of This Century Gallery along with its accompanying furniture. Resembling the amoebas in reliefs by Hans Arp, their free-ranging form accommodated similarly free-

ranging functions, whether as rocking chairs for gallery visitors or bases for works of art.

DISSOLUTION AND TRANSPARENCY
If the influence of designers like Rietveld, Breuer, and Aalto, or Kiesler, Saarinen, and the Eameses, is to thank for the fact that the furnishing of modern households has become "'cleaner in line and lighter in mass",[33] the radicalism of their solutions can be attributed to technical achievements as well as to a dialogue with the various abstract, concrete, surrealist, and conceptual tendencies in art. These tendencies intensified following the Second World War and repeatedly called into question the boundaries separating the disciplines. And, of course, it also goes without saying that art, in turn, responded to the scientific and technical innovations that transformed our conception of the world.

griff im Jahr darauf auch der Architekt Mart Stam zum Stahlrohr. Ermutigt von einer dem Holz weit überlegenen Stabilität entwickelte er aus einer einzigen Schlaufe des Materials den ersten Stuhl, dessen Sitz nur von Vorderbeinen getragen wird – ein Konzept, das Mies van der Rohe kurzerhand zum elegant geschwungenen und nun tatsächlich federnden Freischwinger verbesserte. Überhaupt leistete „Mies, der bis ins Letzte mit den selbstreferentiellen Poetiken der Moderne konform ging"[37], seinen größten Beitrag zu Design und Architektur weniger durch grundlegende Neuerungen als durch ein beharrliches Sublimieren derselben. Doch während ihn die äußerste Präzision, mit der er an ästhetischen Auflösungen der Masse feilte, zu einem Schutzheiligen der minimalistischen Kunst machte, wurden seine einflussreichen Formulierungen, etwa die der gläsernen Wand, von der Architektur eines Internationalen Stils gnadenlos ausgeschlachtet. Und wo bei Mies der Blick noch gerichtet wurde, rauschte er bei seinen Epigonen geradewegs durchs Haus hindurch oder prallte an der Spiegelung ihrer Glasfassaden brüsk ab.

Als in den 1960er Jahren die flimmernden Leinwände der Op-Art dem Betrachter den Boden unter den Füßen wegzogen, kam man mit neuen durchsichtigen Kunststoffen dem Ziel der Entmaterialisierung auch in der Einrichtung einen Schritt näher. „Es ist der unbesetzte Platz, der ein Zimmer be-

wohnbar macht", zitierte Bernard Rudofsky weiland den chinesischen Schriftsteller Lin Yutang,[38] und Breuers Vision, eines Tages auf einer Luftsäule sitzen zu können, wurde mit *Blow*, dem ersten aufblasbaren Wohnmöbel, zur Realität. Oder war man da einer Täuschung aufgesessen und einen Schritt zu weit gegangen? Sollten die Fantasien von Teleportation, wie sie Joe Colombos *Acrilica*-Leuchte in Gang setzte, doch Science-Fiction bleiben? Jedenfalls wurde der Wegwerfgesellschaft mit der Ölkrise 1973 ein erster kräftiger Strich durch die Rechnung gemacht. In einem Rückblick auf sein Werk konfrontierte uns der japanische Designer Shiro Kuramata stattdessen mit folgendem Konflikt: „Das Nichts regiert alles", aber „die Gravitation ist eine Kraft, die über uns steht und alle Dinge auf Erden kontrolliert [...] einschließlich der Ideologien".[39] Einen so überraschenden (und nicht zu widerlegenden) Widerspruch, der symptomatisch für den Dualismus in der shintoistischen Ethik und Ästhetik ist, verstand Kuramata mit seinen Möbeln in poetischen Verbindungen aus Transparenz und Schwerkraft immer wieder aufzuheben, wofür er von vielen Kollegen bis heute verehrt wird.

Richard Buckminster Fuller, *Geodesic Dome* für den Pavillon der Vereinigten Staaten bei der Expo 1967 in Montreal, Foto: Robert Nachbargauer.

Richard Buckminster Fuller, *Geodesic Dome* for the U.S. Pavillon, Expo 1967 in Montreal, photograph: Robert Nachbargauer.

The overturning of once unshakeably held fundamental postulates— as shown in the motif of freely gliding volumes in space in Wright's, Malevich's, and Rietveld's creations, as well as in El Lissitzky's *Proun* installations, which were articulated as "transfer stations on the path towards new buildings that can be conceived as 'floating'"[34]—was always additionally meant to free man from his constraints using basic means in order to institute a new balance. Accordingly, the dissolution of matter, the beauty of light, and the control of energy were recurrent themes in the imposing monuments that were staged for world's fairs and other international expositions: Joseph Paxton's *Crystal Palace* in London (1851), the *Eiffel Tower* in Paris (1889), Mies van der Rohe's *Barcelona Pavilion* (1929), the *Atomium* in Brussels (1958), Richard Buckminster Fuller's *Geodesic Dome* in

Montreal (1967), and Peter Zumthor's *Klangkörper* in Hannover (2000).

In the twentieth century, the technical possibilities for exhausting the efficiency of materials—as an economic and now, above all, ecological concern— were hugely expanded or, in other cases, substituted with alternatives whose aim was to intelligently outsmart matter and achieve the desired effects with mere electricity, radio waves, and radiation. This has long established itself as an everyday reality that compels designers and architects in all fields to increasingly work together with engineers. Yet a revolution already occurred back in 1925 at the Bauhaus with Marcel Breuer's discovery of tubular steel as a material for domestic use. Adhering to Walter Gropius' precept of "the machine as the most modern means of design"[35] and

impressed by the stability of his new bicycle, Breuer designed the *Wassily* as an armchair cut down to its frame. The Bauhaus portrayed his creation as the final stage victory of a systematic reduction of material before achieving the ultimate possibility of sitting on "an elastic column of air".[36] Compared with Rietveld's *Roodblauwe Stoel*, it constitutes an even more advanced dematerialization, with the machine-like frame constructed from reflective tubes gliding over the floor and the seat, back, and armrests made from metallically glimmering bands of fabric.

The year after El Lissitzky published his bold concept for buildings weightlessly projecting into the lofty heights (*Wolkenbügel*, "Cloud-Hangers"), architect Mart Stam likewise turned to tubular steel. Emboldened by the material's superior stability to wood, he employed a single steel loop to create the first chair with

ZEICHEN UND VORBILD

Wie Kuramata, so spürte auch der Designer Ettore Sottsass, mit dem er in der Gruppe Memphis zusammengearbeitet hatte, den wechselnden metaphorischen Bildern unserer „erscheinungssüchtigen Epoche"[40] nach. Sottsass ging es um die Botschaften, die seine Objekte aussenden, als reflexive Beziehung zwischen dem Gegenstand und seinem Gegenüber, der weit mehr ist als sein Benutzer. Mit der Forderung des Schweizer Künstlers und Designers Max Bill nach einer optimierten, bleibenden Schönheit, so „dass sie gleichermassen eine funktion sei"[41], ist Sottsass' Ansatz also sicher nicht zu verwechseln. Konfrontiert mit dem Vorwurf der Kurzlebigkeit einer solchen Gestaltung, deren Schwergewicht sich von der funktionalen Praxis auf den ästhetischen Effekt verlagert, antwortete er: „Wenn eine Gesellschaft den Werteverlust plant, dann ist das einzig nachhaltige Design eines, das mit Werteverlust zu tun hat […]. Das einzig nicht bleibende Design ist eins, das in solch einer Gesellschaft nach Metaphysik sucht, das nach dem Absoluten, der Ewigkeit sucht."[42] Eine so dezidiert postmoderne Einstellung zum Design als Medium der Kommunikation bedeutet jedoch keinen Verzicht auf Effizienz und Reduktion. Die Objekte der Gruppe Memphis, die hier nur stellvertretend für einen grundsätzlichen Ansatz im Industriedesign genannt seien, sind effizient insofern, als sich hier die Sprache zum Zeichen verdichtet. Aber auch produktionstechnisch wurde diesem Ansatz damals entsprochen, da eine Massenproduktion in der Regel gar nicht erst versucht wurde, sondern Einzelstücke in den Tischlereien außerhalb Mailands aus billigen Pressspanplatten und Laminat zusammengebaut wurden.

Die trivialen, der Populärkultur entlehnten Motive und das Infragestellen von Wirklichkeitsebenen wurde Memphis oft als Rückgriff auf Strategien der Pop-Art ausgelegt. Betrachtet man den Dialog von Kunst und Design jedoch historisch, kann man beobachten, dass die Kunst im Vergleich zur Warenästhetik strategisch hinterherhinkte und erst mit Beginn der Pop-Art Mitte der 1950er Jahre anfing, sich für deren Semantik zu interessieren. Das Design hatte sich, wie oben beschrieben, künstlerische Strategien schon viel früher angeeignet – ein Umstand, dem schon die Einrichtung der Designabteilung des MoMA 1930 Rechnung trug. Allerdings hat Design in puncto Semantik auch einen entscheidenden Vorteil gegenüber der Kunst, da die Funktion eines Gebrauchsgegenstands üblicherweise vorausgesetzt ist und es inhaltlich nur noch um die Ausgestaltung dieser Botschaft geht. Ein Stuhl ist immer auch ein zeichenhafter Stellvertreter des Menschen und, mehr noch, des Sitzens, und eine Leuchte ist schon immer ein symbolischer Stellvertreter des Lichts. Eine Herausforderung, um nicht zu sagen eine Kunst, besteht für den Designer also darin, etwas über die Art des Sitzens, des Leuchtens, des Fahrens, Öffnens usw. auszusagen und mithin eben die Beziehung zwischen Objekt und Benutzer zu gestalten. Nach Effizienz sucht diese Gestaltung nicht zuletzt in einem kleinsten gemeinsamen

----

a seat supported solely by the front legs—a concept that Mies van der Rohe quickly improved upon in his elegantly swinging and now truly flexible cantilevered model. In general, "Mies, always consistent with the modernist poetics of self-referentiality",[37] made his greatest contribution to design and architecture less through fundamental innovations than through persistent sublimation of such. Yet while the extreme precision with which he refined aesthetic dissolutions of mass made him a patron saint of minimalist art, his influential formulations, such as the glass wall, were mercilessly exploited by International Style architecture. And while the angle of view was carefully aligned in the case of Mies, it whooshed straight through the buildings of his imitators, or brusquely ricocheted off the reflection of their glass facades.

While the flickering canvases of 1960s Op Art pulled the rug out from underneath the viewer, furnishing took its own step towards the goal of dematerialization with new transparent plastics. "It is the unoccupied space which makes a room inhabitable", as Bernard Rudofsky once quoted the Chinese writer Lin Yutang,[38] and Breuer's vision of some day being able to sit on a column of air became a reality with *Blow*, the first piece of inflatable furnishing for the home. Yet, was it a fool's bargain that was struck, taking things one step too far? Could it really be that the fantasies of teleportation, as suggested by Joe Colombo's *Acrylica* lamp, were to remain in the realm of science fiction after all? In any case, the throwaway society experienced its first shock with the 1973 oil crisis.

In a retrospective look at his work, the Japanese designer Shiro Kuramata instead confronts us with the following conflict: "nothingness rules over everything" but "gravitation is a force that stands over us and keeps all things on this earth under its control ... including ideology".[39] Symptomatic of the dualism in the Shinto ethic and aesthetic, this surprising (and irrefutable) contradiction was skilfully resolved by Kuramata time and again in his furniture, with its poetic compounds of transparency and gravity, for which he continues to be venerated by many colleagues up to the present day.

SIGN AND MODEL

Like his fellow Memphis collaborator Kuramata, Ettore Sottsass also sought to trace the changing metaphorical imagery of our "appearance-addicted epoch".[40] Sottsass was concerned with the messages his objects sent out as a reflexive relationship between the object and its counterpart, which is something much greater than just its user. Such an approach is a far cry from the call made by Swiss artist and designer Max Bill for an optimized lasting beauty that would be "equally a

Nenner von Rationalität und Emotionalität – und zwar möglichst noch bevor das Objekt gekauft ist. Besonders deutlich wird diese Herausforderung bei technischen Geräten, deren Funktionsfülle gar nicht mehr abgebildet werden kann. Während hier die Stars der heute vorgeblichen Zukunft die Interfaces der Firma Apple sind, war Dieter Rams mit seinen Geräten für Braun ein überragender Pionier in dieser Kunst der Reduktion.

„Toast has a happy shape" schreibt der japanische Designer Naoto Fukasawa,[43] und wenn man die Geräte von Braun mit denen von Apple vergleicht, stellt man überrascht fest, dass alle aussehen wie Toast. Jedenfalls haben alle eine rechtwinklige, flache Grundform mit abgerundeten Ecken, die eben keine Ecken sind und uns auch wohl deshalb ein Lächeln auf die Lippen zaubern. Die Kombination aus rationaler Geradlinigkeit, wie sie die Industrieproduktion bevorzugt, und der auf einen Viertelkreis reduzierten, sinnlichen Rundung verschmilzt Gefühl und Verstand zu einem Zeichen, das uns nicht erst beim Berühren, sondern schon beim Betrachten mit der Technik versöhnt, denn „man *sieht* es nicht mit den Augen, sondern man *berührt* es mit den Augen"[44]. Die emotionale Verbundenheit mit einem Objekt bezeichnet die japanische Sprache mit dem Begriff *aichaku*: „Es ist eine im Animismus wurzelnde Art symbiotischer Liebe zu einem Objekt, das Zuneigung nicht nur für das verdient, was es tut, sondern für das, was es ist. Wenn wir anerkennen, dass es *aichaku* in unserer gestalteten Umwelt gibt, können wir uns besser um das Design von Gegenständen bemühen, die bei den Menschen dreierlei hervorrufen: Gefühle, Fürsorge und den Wunsch, sie ein Leben lang zu besitzen."[45] Während dieser Wunsch von den nachfolgenden Generationen elektronischer Geräte mit Sicherheit schnell enttäuscht wird, sollten sich *aichaku* also vor allem Designer von Gütern längerfristiger Investitionen zu Herzen nehmen.

ABBILD

Einen wichtigen Anteil an der Reduktion im Design hatte schließlich die Fotografie, denn seit ihrer Verbreitung in der ersten Hälfte des 19. Jahrhunderts diente sie nicht in erster Linie einer objektiven, sondern einer ökonomischen Wiedergabe von Motiven sowie der Vervielfältigung von Bildern. Die Bilder, die wir uns von der Welt und ihren Gegenständen machen, sind, heute mehr denn je, von fremden – fotografischen oder filmischen – Perspektiven geprägt. Beim Entwurf eines Gegenstands dienen solche Aufnahmen dazu, entweder den Schaffensprozess zu dokumentieren oder die Idee vom Urheber zu distanzieren, um sie objektiver betrachten zu können. In jedem Fall machen sie Details sichtbar, die dem Auge und der Erkenntnis ansonsten verborgen blieben,[46] – was erst recht für reduzierte Formen gilt, denen man kleinste Fehler sofort ansieht. Obwohl diese Bilder also unsere Erkenntnisse über Design und dessen Entwicklungen fördern, verlängern sie zugleich die Vergangenheit und multiplizieren sie schließlich so oft, dass sie uns als Bilderflut zu überwältigen dro-

----

function".[41] Confronted with the charge of ephemerality for such designs whose weight shifts from functional practice to aesthetic effect, Sottsass replied: "If a society plans obsolescence, the only possible enduring design is one that deals with that obsolescence.... The only design that does not endure is the one that in such a society looks for metaphysics, looks for the absolute, for eternity."[42] Such a decidedly postmodern take on design as a medium of communication does not, however, mean a complete renunciation of efficiency and reduction. The objects of the Memphis group, cited here as examples of a basic approach in industrial design, are efficient insofar as their language becomes concentrated into a sign. This approach was additionally reflected in the production process. In most cases, mass production was never even attempted, with one-off pieces instead being assembled from cheap pressboard and laminate in joinery workshops outside Milan.

The trivial motifs Memphis borrowed from popular culture and its questioning of levels of reality were often construed as being borrowed from strategies of Pop Art. Yet when examining the dialogue between art and design from a historical perspective, art can be seen as strategically lagging behind the aesthetics of commodities, not becoming interested in its semantics until the emergence of Pop Art in the mid-1950s. As described above, design was much quicker to appropriate the strategies of art—a circumstance manifested in the establishment of the design department at the Museum of Modern Art in New York back in 1930. Admittedly, design maintains a decisive advantage over art in regard to semantics, as the function of articles of daily use is typically predetermined and the only remaining content-related matter is the articulation of a message. A chair always acts as a figurative surrogate for the individual and, what is more, for sitting, and a lamp always serves as a symbolic proxy for light. The challenge, not to say the art, of the designer thus consists in saying something about the nature of sitting, lighting, driving, opening, and so forth, and hence to shape and define the relationship between object and user. Such designs are apt to seek efficiency in the lowest common denominator of rationality and emotionality—with this, preferably, firmly established before the object is purchased. The challenge becomes particularly apparent in technical devices whose scope of functions can no longer be depicted. And while today the interfaces of Apple devices appear as the stars of a hypothetical future, Dieter Rams was an exceptionally accomplished pioneer in this art of reduction with the electrical appliances he designed for Braun.

"Toast has a happy shape", writes

hen. Den praktischen Umgang mit den Dingen kann uns letztlich aber selbst in Fragen der Optik kein Bild ersetzen. Max Bill interessierten in seiner Lehre „Erfahrungs- und Ermessensfragen", die „harmonische Führung einer Kurve" und die „genaue Ausbalancierung von Proportion und Volumen, die ebenso wichtig sind wie die reine Funktion",[47] denn die Kunst der Reduktion ist letztlich eine Schule des Sehens: Sie trainiert ein unvoreingenommenes Sehen ohne Regeln.

----

the Japanese designer Naoto Fukasawa,[43] and when comparing the products of Braun and Apple, it is striking how they all do look like toast. At least they all have a flat, orthogonal basic form, with rounded corners that, as a matter of fact, are no corners at all—which might just be the reason for their particular appeal. Rational straight lines preferred by industrial production are thus combined with sensual curvature, abbreviated to the quarter-circle of rounded corners. This fuses sense and sensibility into a sign that reconciles us with technology not only at the moment of touch but already upon viewing, for "you're not looking at it with your eyes,... you're touching it with your eyes".[44] The emotional connection with an object is described by the Japanese term *aichaku*: "It is a kind of symbiotic love for an object that deserves affection not for what it does, but for what it is. Acknowledging the existence of *aichaku*

in our built environment helps us to aspire to design artifacts that people will feel for, care for, and own for a lifetime."[45] While this desire will surely be quickly disappointed by subsequent generations of electronic devices, *aichaku* should be especially taken to heart in the design of goods requiring long-term investments.

IMAGE
Finally, an important contribution to reduction in design has been rendered by photography. Since its dissemination in the first half of the nineteenth century, the medium has primarily revolved around the economical reproduction of motifs and duplication of images rather than objectivity. Today more than ever, the images we create for ourselves of the world and its objects are defined by the perspectives of others through photography and film. In design, these images serve both to document the creative

process and to enable the designer to distance himself from his creation in order to view it with greater objectivity. Through them, details that would otherwise remain hidden to the eye and elude realization become visible[46]—which is all the more true for reduced forms in which the slightest flaws become instantly apparent. Yet, although these photographs further our knowledge of design and its development, they simultaneously prolong the past and multiply it to the point of overwhelming us with a flood of images. In his teachings, Max Bill was interested in "questions that have to do with experience and judgment", "tracing a harmonic curve", and the "exact balancing of proportion and volume", which he found "just as important as pure function".[47] For in the end, the art of reduction is a school of seeing, training us to develop unbiased perception without rules.

1 Ludwig Mies van der Rohe hatte diesen berühmten Grundsatz von seinem Lehrer Peter Behrens übernommen. Vgl. *Four Great Makers of Modern Architecture: Gropius, Le Corbusier, Mies van der Rohe, Wright. A Verbatim Record of a Symposium Held at the School of Architecture from March to May 1961*, New York 1963, S. 129.

2 George Nelson: „Zum Design von Sportgeräten", in: *Du*, Nr. 425,1976, S. 28.

3 Karl Marx: *Das Kapital. Kritik der politischen Ökonomie*, Erster Band, Marx-Engels-Werke, Berlin 1977, Bd. 23, S. 85.

4 Ebd., S. 49.

5 Abgeschieden von den Neuerungen der Zivilisation verarbeitete im 18. und 19. Jahrhundert die religiöse Gemeinschaft der Shaker lokale Naturmaterialen zu vereinfachten, funktionalisierten und typisierten Gebrauchsgegenständen.

6 Isaac Newton: „Fragments from a Treatise on Revelation", Manuskript, publ. in Frank E. Manuel: *The Religion of Isaac Newton*, Oxford 1974, S. 120, zit. nach: Stephen David Snobelen: „Isaac Newton, Socinianism and 'the One Supreme God'", in: Martin Mulsow, Jan Rohls (Hrsg.): *Socinianism and Arminianism: Antitrinitarians, Calvinists, and Cultural Exchange in Seventeenth-Century Europe*, Leiden, Boston, Tokio 2005, S. 273.

7 Alexander von Humboldt: *Kosmos. Entwurf einer physischen Weltbeschreibung*, Einleitende Betrachtungen, Frankfurt a. M. 2004, S.10. Vgl. Wolfgang Häusler: „Versuch über die Einfachheit oder: Die Ordnung der Vielfalt in Politik, Bildung und Kunst der bürgerlichen Gesellschaft", in: *Biedermeier. Die Erfindung der Einfachheit*, hrsg. v. Hans Ottomeyer et.al., Aust.-Kat. Albertina, Wien, DHM, Berlin, Louvre, Paris, Ostfildern 2006, S. 115.

8 Häusler, ebd.

9 Die Form der weltweit unabhängig voneinander entstandenen Pyramiden wurde vermutlich von Sonnenstrahlen abgeleitet, die durch die Wolken brechen. Neben den Gestirnen und dem Meereshorizont ist dies eins der wenigen Naturphänomene, das so exakt und wohl auch deswegen voller Symbolik erscheint.

10 Nikolaus Pevsner: „Design und Industrie im Laufe der Geschichte", in: ders.: *Architektur und Design. Von der Romantik zur Sachlichkeit*, München 1971, S. 226.

11 Hermine Wittgenstein: „Mein Bruder Ludwig", zit. in: Bernhard Leitner: *The architecture of Ludwig Wittgenstein. A Documentation, with Exerzpts from the Family Recollections by Hermine Wittgenstein*, Halifax und London, 1973, S. 29, zit. nach: Walter Kugler: „Sprache – Seele – Raum. Rudolf Steiner und Ludwig Wittgenstein", in: *Archiskulptur*, hrsg. v. Markus Brüderlin, Ausst.-Kat. Fondation Beyeler Basel, Ostfildern-Ruit, 2004, S. 128.

12 Zit. nach Kugler, ebd.

13 George Nelson in: *How to See*, Boston, Toronto 1977, S. 112. Zit. nach: Stanley Abercrombie: „George Nelson zum Lesen", in: *George Nelson. Architekt. Autor. Designer. Lehrer*, hrsg. v. Jochen Eisenbrand und Alexander von Vegesack, Ausst.-Kat. Vitra Design Museum, Weil am Rhein 2008, S. 35. Vgl. auch die Schweizer Zeitschrift *DU*, a.a.O., S. 28 (Vgl. Anm. 2).

14 Ivan Margolius: *Automobiles by Architects*, London 2000, 48.

15 Ebd.

16 Die „sparsame Verwendung von Material", den „Umgang mit Volumen und Raum" und „die geniale Bauweise" hatte Le Corbusier nicht zuletzt an einem um 1925 hergestellten Plattenspieler mit Handkurbel bewundert, dem so genannten *Mikiphone*, der in einer Dose von nur 4 cm Höhe und mit einem Durchmesser von 11,5 cm Platz fand. Vgl. Le Corbusier: *Almanach d'architecture moderne*, Paris 1925, S. 197, zit. nach: Lotte Schilder, „Präzisionsindustrie: Miniaturisierung und L'Art Décoratif Moderne", in: *L'Esprit Nouveau*, hrsg. v. Stanislaus von Moos, Ausst.-Kat. Museum für Gestaltung, Zürich 1987, S. 269.

17 „Dem Halbnomaden des heutigen Wirtschaftslebens bringt die Standarisierung seines Wohnungs-[...]bedarfs lebenwichtige Freizügigkeit, Wirtschaftlichkeit, Vereinfachung und Entspannung. Die Höhe unserer Standardisierung ist ein Index unserer Gemeinwirtschaft." Hannes Meyer: „Die neue Welt", in: *Das Werk*, 13. Jg. 1926, Nr. 7, S. 223, zit. nach: Arthur Rüegg: „Die Schweizerische Entwicklung 1925-1935", in: *Schweizer Typenmöbel 1925-1935. Siegfried Giedion und die Wohnbedarf AG*, hrsg. v. Friederike Mehlau-Wiebking et.al., Zürich 1989, S. 13.

18 Gerrit Thomas Rietveld, zit. nach: Theo van Doesburg: „Aanteekeningen bij een leunstoel van Rietveld", in: *De Stijl* 2, Nr. 11, 1919, Beilage XXII; übersetzt vom Autor.

19 Der berühmte Ausspruch Louis Sullivans „form follows function", der zum Leitsatz der Arts-and-Crafts-Bewegung wurde, hat in dieser Japan-Begeisterung vermutlich seinen eigentlichen Ursprung.

20 Wright baute auf die Methoden des Pädagogen Friedrich Fröbel, die ihm seine Mutter vermittelt hatte. Vgl. David Hanks: „Frank Lloyd Wright als Innenarchitekt und seine europäischen Zeitgenossen", in: *Frank Lloyd Wright. Die Lebendige Stadt*, hrsg. v. David G. De Long, Ausst.-Kat. Vitra Design Museum, Weil am Rhein 1998, S. 296.

---

1 Ludwig Mies van der Rohe adopted this famous tenet from his mentor Peter Behrens. See Trustees of Columbia University, *Four Great Makers of Modern Architecture: Gropius, Le Corbusier, Mies van der Rohe, Wright*, the verbatim record of a symposium held at the School of Architecture, Columbia University, March–May 1961 (New York: Da Capo Press, 1970), 129.

2 George Nelson, „Zum Design von Sportgeräten", *Du* 425 (1976), 28.

3 Karl Marx, *Capital: A Critque of Political Economy*, Vol. 1, trans. Ben Fowkes (London: Penguin, 1976), 165.

4 Ibid., 125.

5 Isolated from the innovations of civilization in the eighteenth and nineteenth centuries, the religious community of the Shakers processed local natural materials into simplified, functionalized, and standardized articles of daily use.

6 Isaac Newton, „Fragments from a Treatise on Revelation", a manuscript published in Frank E. Manuel, *The Religion of Isaac Newton* (Oxford: Clarendon Press, 1974), 120.

7 Alexander von Humboldt, *Cosmos: A Sketch of a Physical Description of the Universe*, Vol. 1, trans. E. C. Otté (Baltimore: Johns Hopkins University Press, 1997), 24. See, also, Wolfgang Häusler, „Versuch über die Einfachheit, oder: die Ordnung der Vielfalt in Politik, Bildung und Kunst der bürgerlichen Gesellschaft", in *Biedermeier: Die Erfindung der Einfachheit*, ed. Hans Ottomeyer et al. (Ostfildern: Hatje Cantz Verlag, 2006).

8 Häusler, „Versuch über die Einfachheit", 115.

9 Created independent from one another, the form of the pyramids in various locations around the world was presumably derived from the rays of the sun descending through the clouds. Along with the stars and the horizon of the sea, this is one of the few natural phenomena that appears with such precise clarity, which is probably what imbues it with so much symbolism.

10 Nikolaus Pevsner, „Design and Industry through the Ages", in *Studies in Art, Architecture, and Design: Victorian and After* (London: Thames & Hudson, 1968), 16.

11 Hermine Wittgenstein, „My Brother Ludwig", in *Recollections of Wittgenstein*, ed. Rush Rhees (Oxford: Oxford University Press, 1984), 6.

12 Ludwig Wittgenstein, *Culture and Value: A Selection from the Posthumous Remains* (Oxford: Blackwell, 1998 [1980]), 43e, as quoted in Paul Smith, „Real Primitives: Cezanne, Wittgenstein, and the Nature of Aesthetic Quality", in *Value, Art, Politics: Criticism, Meaning and Interpretation after Postmodernism*, ed. Jonathan Harris (Liverpool: Liverpool University Press, 2007), 98.

13 George Nelson, *How to See: Visual Adventures in a World God Never Made* (Boston: Little Brown, 1977), 112. See, also, Nelson, „Zum Design von Sportgeräten".

14 Ivan Margolius, *Automobiles by Architects* (London: Wiley-Academy, 2000), 48.

15 Ibid.

16 Similarly, Le Corbusier had especially admired the „sparing use of material", the „handling of volume and space", and „the ingenious construction" of a hand-cranked phonograph—the so-called *Mikiphone*—manufactured around 1925 and housed in a case just four centimetres high with a diameter of 11.5 centimetres. See Le Corbusier, *Almanach d'architecture moderne* (Paris: Crès, 1925), 197, quoted in Lotte Schilder, „Präzisionsindustrie: Miniaturisierung und L'Art Décoratif Moderne", in *L'Esprit Nouveau: Le Corbusier und die Industrie, 1920–1925*, ed. Stanislaus von Moos, exhibition catalogue (Zurich: Museum für Gestaltung Zürich, 1987), 269.

17 „Because of the standardization of his needs as regards housing..., the semi-nomad of our modern productive system has the benefit of freedom of movement, economies, simplification and relaxation, all of which are vitally important for him. The degree of our standardization is an index of our communal productive system." Hannes Meyer, „Die neue Welt", *Das Werk* 13, no. 7 (1926), 223, translated by K. Michael Hays, *Modernism and the Posthumanist Subject: The Architecture of Hannes Meyer and Ludwig Hilberseimer* (Cambridge, MA: MIT Press, 1995), 65.

18 Gerrit Thomas Rietveld, as quoted in Theo van Doesburg, „Aanteekeningen bij een leunstoel van Rietveld", *De Stijl* 2, no. 11 (1919), insert XXII.

19 The famous saying by Louis Sullivan that „form follows function", which became a guiding principle of the Arts and Crafts movement, presumably originated in this fascination with Japan.

20 Wright built on the methods of the educator Friedrich Fröbel, which had been conveyed to him early on by his mother. See David Hanks, „The Decorative Designs of Frank Lloyd Wright and His European Contemporaries", in *Frank Lloyd Wright and the Living City*, ed. David De Long, exhibition catalogue (Weil am Rhein: Vitra Design Museum, 1998), 296.

21 As commonly seen in *ukiyo-e* prints, the representational nature of Wright's drawings is intensified

21 Wie in manchen *Ukiyo-e*-Drucken wird die Präsenz der Darstellung gesteigert, indem die Rahmen der Zeichnungen partiell unterbrochen sind und in die Motive übergehen.

22 Vgl. D. Hanks, a.a.O., S. 295 (vgl. Anm. 21).

23 Vor allem trifft dies für die Möbel im Larkin-Gebäude und im Haus für Avery Coonley zu.

24 van Doesburg, a.a.O. (vgl. Anm. 19).

25 Le Corbusier in: *Vers une Architecture*, Paris 1923, zit. nach: Christina Lodder: „Searching for Utopia", in: *Modernism: Designing a New World 1914–1939*, hrsg. v. Christopher Wilk, Ausst.-Kat. Victoria and Albert Museum, London 2006, S. 33; übersetzt vom Autor.

26 Christof Kübler: „Tracés Régulateurs", in: von Moos: *L'Esprit Nouveau*, a.a.O., S. 179 (vgl. Anm. 15).

27 Vgl. Eva B. Ottillinger: *Adolf Loos. Wohnkonzepte und Möbelentwürfe*, Wien 1994, S. 15.

28 Le Corbusier: *Almanach d'architecture moderne*, zit. nach Stanislaus van Moos: „Thonet", in: ders. (Hrsg), a.a.O., S. 277 (vgl. Anm. 17).

29 Überliefert sind von 1874 das amerikanische Patent eines Stuhls, bei der ein einziges Sperrholzbrett von der Lehne über den Sitz bis zu den Vorderfüßen gebogen ist, und nach demselben Prinzip ein Prototyp von August Thonet um 1900.

30 Ray Eames schöpfte aus ihrer Ausbildung an Hans Hofmanns New Yorker Kunstschule und aus ihren profunden Kenntnissen im zeitgenössischen Tanz.

31 Brâncusi wiederum hatte schon seine *Colonne sans fin* von 1918 auch als Architekturmodell gesehen. Kiesler, der zeitlebens auch als Bühnenbildner arbeitete, kam durch den Erfolg seines „elektro-

mechanischen" Bühnenbilds 1923 für ein Stück von Karel Capek in Berlin in Kontakt mit Theo van Doesburg, El Lissitzky und anderen Vertretern der künstlerischen Avantgarde.

32 Funktional gehört in diese Reihe eigentlich noch das verdichtete, ganz auf die Bedürfnisse der Bewohner zugeschnittene Gefüge der von Adolf Loos 1928–1930 in Prag gebauten *Villa Müller*, die nach außen den strengen Quader eines mittelalterlichen Wohnturms zeigt.

33 Herbert J. Gans: „Design and the Consumer: A View of the Sociology and Culture of ‚Good Design'", in: *Design since 1945*, hrsg. v. Kathryn B. Hiesinger, Ausst.-Kat. Philadelphia Museum of Art, Philadelphia 1983, S. 35; übersetzt vom Autor.

34 Franz Meyer: „Transform-Station", in: *Transform*, hrsg. v. Theodora Vischer, Ausst.-Kat. Kunstmuseum Basel, Basel 1992, S. 9.

35 Walter Gropius: *Idee und Aufbau des Staatlichen Bauhauses*, in: *Staatliches Bauhaus Weimar 1919–1923*, hrsg, v. Staatlichen Bauhaus und Karl Nierendorf, München 1980, S. 12 (Reprint der Ausgabe 1923).

36 *bauhaus*, Nr. 1, 1926, S. 3. Schon zwölf Jahre zuvor hatte Marcel Duchamp die Auswahl von Gegenständen zur Kunst erklärt und in einem Readymadedie Assoziation von Möbel und Fahrrad in die Welt gesetzt.

37 Bruno Reichlin: „Technisches Denken, Denktechniken", in: *Jean Prouvé – Die Poetik des technischen Objekts*, hrsg. v. Alexander von Vegesack, Ausst.-Kat. Vitra Design Museum, Weil am Rhein 2005, S. 39.

38 Bernard Rudofsky: *Behind the Picture Window*, New York 1955, S. 175; übersetzt vom Autor.

39 *Shiro Kuramata. 1934–1991*, hrsg. v. Michiko Aikawa, Ausst.-Kat. Hara Museum of Contemporary Art, Tokio 1996, S. 153 u. S. 140.

40 Thomas Kellein: „Die Konsumgesellschaft als himmlische Stadt", in Vischer, a.a.O., S. 209 (vgl. Anm. 36).

41 Max Bill: „Schönheit aus Funktion und als Funktion", in: *Werk*, Nr. 8, 1949, S. 272, zit. nach: Claude Lichtenstein: *Theorie und Praxis der guten Form. Max Bill und das Design*. Kunstmuseum Winterthur und Gewerbemuseum Winterthur, Zürich 2008, S. 148.

42 Ettore Sottsass in: „Design and Theory. Two Points of View", in: Hiesinger, a.a.O., S. 3; übersetzt vom Autor (vgl. Anm. 35).

43 Naoto Fukasawa und Tamotsu Fujii: *The Outline. The Unseen Outline of Things*, Ausst.-Kat. 21_21 Design Sight, Tokio 2009, S. 106.

44 Ebd., S. 92.

45 John Maeda: *The Laws of Simplicity*, Cambridge, Mass. 2006, S. 69f.

46 Charles Eames nutzte die Fotografie nicht nur zur Dokumentation, sondern auch zur „Objektivierung" der Entwicklung dreidimensionaler Arbeiten. Konsequent fotografierte er selbst seine dreidimensionalen Studien in verschiedenen Entwicklungsstadien und aus unterschiedlichen Blickwinkeln, um vom realen Gegenstand auf ein neutrales Bild zu abstrahieren.

47 Max Bill: „Erfahrungswerte bei der Formgestaltung von Industrieprodukten", in: *Werk*, Nr. 5, 1946, S. 170, zit. nach Claude Lichtenstein, a.a.O, S. 154 (vgl. Anm. 43).

----

in the way the frame occasionally merges with the depicted motifs.

22 See Hanks, "The Decorative Designs of Frank Lloyd Wright", 295.

23 This is especially apparent in the furniture of the Larkin Building and the Avery Coonley House.

24 Theo van Doesburg, "Aanteekeningen bij een leunstoel van Rietveld".

25 Le Corbusier, *Towards a New Architecture*, trans. Frederick Etchells (London: Payson & Clarke, 1927), 199, quoted in Christina Lodder, "Searching for Utopia", in *Modernism: Designing a New World, 1914–1939*, ed. Christopher Wilk, exhibition catalogue (London: Victoria and Albert Museum, 2006), 33.

26 Christof Kübler, "Tracés Régulateurs", in Stanislaus von Moos (ed.), *L'Esprit Nouveau*, 179.

27 See Eva B. Ottillinger, *Adolf Loos: Wohnkonzepte u. Möbelentwürfe* (Vienna: Residenz Verlag, 1994), 15.

28 Le Corbusier, *Almanach d'architecture moderne*, 145–6, quoted in Stanislaus von Moos, "Thonet", in his (ed.), *L'Esprit Nouveau*, 277.

29 An American patent surviving from 1874 proposes a chair bent from a single board of plywood, from the back through the seat down to the front legs—a principle that also featured in a prototype by August Thonet from around 1900.

30 Ray Eames drew from her training at Hans Hofmann's school of art in New York, as well as from her profound knowledge of contemporary dance.

31 Brâncusi, in turn, considered his *Colonne sans fin* from 1918 also as an architectural model. A theatre designer throughout his life, Kiesler came in contact with Theo van Doesburg, El Lissitzky, and other mem-

bers of the artistic avant-garde through the success of his "electro-mechanical" stage set for a 1923 play by Karel Capek in Berlin.

32 In terms of function, this lineage of works also includes the condensed structure of *Villa Müller*, built by Adolf Loos in Prague between 1928 and 1930. Perfectly adapted to the needs of its occupants on the inside, it outwardly presents the austere cuboid of a medieval tower house.

33 Herbert J. Gans, "Design and the Consumer: A View of the Sociology and Culture of 'Good Design'", in *Design Since 1945*, ed. Kathryn B. Hiesinger, exhibition catalogue (Philadelphia: Philadelphia Museum of Art, 1983), 35.

34 Franz Meyer, "Transform-Station", in *Transform*, ed. Theodora Vischer, exhibition catalogue (Basel: Kunstmuseum Basel, 1992), 9.

35 Walter Gropius, "Idee und Aufbau des Staatlichen Bauhauses", in *Staatliches Bauhaus, Weimar: 1919–1923*, ed. *Staatliches Bauhaus* and Karl Nierendorf (Munich: Kraus, 1980 [1923]), 12.

36 *bauhaus* 1 (1926), 3. Twelve years earlier, Marcel Duchamp had declared the selection of objects to be art and had introduced, with his ready-made, the association of furniture and bicycle.

37 Bruno Reichlin, "Technical Thought, Techniques of Thinking", in *Jean Prouvé: The Poetics of the Technical Object*, ed. Alexander von Vegesack, exhibition catalogue (Weil am Rhein: Vitra Design Museum, 2005), 39.

38 Bernard Rudofsky, *Behind the Picture Window* (New York: Oxford University Press, 1955), 175.

39 *Shiro Kuramata: 1934–1991*, ed. Michiko Aikawa, exhibition catalogue (Tokyo: Hara Museum of Contemporary Art, 1996), 153, 140.

40 Thomas Kellein, "Die Konsumgesellschaft als himmlische Stadt", in Theodora Vischer (ed.), *Transform*, 209.

41 Max Bill, "Schönheit aus Funktion und als Funktion", in *Werk* 8 (1949), 272, translated in René Spitz, *Hfg Ulm: The View Behind the Foreground: The Political History of the Ulm School of Design, 1953–1968* (Stuttgart: Edition Axel Menges, 2002), 64.

42 Ettore Sottsass, "Design and Theory: Two Points of View", in Kathryn B. Hiesinger (ed.), *Design Since 1945*, 3.

43 Naoto Fukasawa and Tamotsu Fujii, *The Outline: The Unseen Outline of Things*, exhibition catalogue (Tokyo: 21_21 Design Sight, 2009), 106.

44 Ibid., 92.

45 John Maeda, *The Laws of Simplicity* (Cambridge, MA: MIT Press, 2006), 69–70.

46 Charles Eames used photography not only for documentation purposes but also for "objectification" of the development of three-dimensional works. He methodically photographed his three-dimensional studies in various stages and from different angles in order to abstract from these real-enough objects a neutral image.

47 Max Bill, "Erfahrungswerte bei der Formgestaltung von Industrieprodukten", *Werk* 5 (1946), 170, translated in René Spitz, *Hfg Ulm*, 64.

FERTIGUNG /
MANUFACTURING

56

57

58

59

60

EINHEIT /
UNITY

61

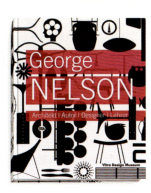

**George NELSON //
Architekt, Autor, Designer,
Lehrer**

Hardcover
Format 23,5 x 28 cm
Seiten / pages 352
300 Abbildungen,
überwiegend farbig
300 pictures,
Herausgeber / Editor:
Alexander von Vegesack,
Jochen Eisenbrand

ISBN 978-3-931936-81-5
Art. Nr. 20052301
(Deutscher / German Text)

**George NELSON //
Architect, Writer, Designer,
Teacher**
ISBN 978-3-931936-82-2
Art. Nr. 20052302
(Englischer / English Text)

**Le Corbusier –
The Art of Architecture**

Hardcover
Format 22 x 31 cm
Seiten / pages 398
500 Abb., davon 233 farbige
und 267 Duplex-Abbildungen /
500 pictures (233 color and
267 duplex-illustrations)
Herausgeber / Editor:
Alexander von Vegesack,
Stanislaus von Moos,
Arthur Rüegg, Mateo Kries

ISBN 978-3-931936-71-6
Art. Nr. 20012101
(Deutscher / German Text)

**Le Corbusier –
The Art of Architecture**
ISBN 978-3-931936-72-3
Art. Nr. 20012102
(Englischer / English Text)

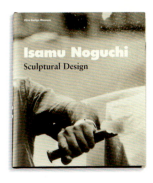

**Isamu Noguchi –
Sculptural Design**

Hardcover
Format 28,5 x 25 cm
Seiten/pages 320
155 Abb. davon 80 farbige
und 75 S/W-Abbildungen /
155 pictures (80 color and
75 b/w-illustrations)
Herausgeber / Editor:
Alexander von Vegesack,
Jochen Eisenbrand,
Katharina V. Posch

ISBN 978-3-931936-33-4
Art. Nr. 20017001
(Deutscher / German Text)

ISBN 978-3-931936-38-9
Art. Nr. 20017003
(Französischer / French Text)

**Jean Prouvé – Die Poetik des
technischen Gegenstandes**

Hardcover
Format 28 x 23 cm
Seiten / pages 393
895 Abb. davon 240 farbige
und 655 Duplex-Abbildungen /
895 pictures (240 color and
655 duplex-illustrations)
Herausgeber / Editor:
Alexander von Vegesack
Mitherausgeber / Co-editor:
Bruno Reichlin
Konzept / conzept:
Catherine Dumont d'Ayot

ISBN 978-3-931936-53-2
Art. Nr. 20018501
(Deutscher / German Text)

**Jean Prouvé – The Poetics
of the Technical Objects**
ISBN 978-3-931936-54-9
Art. Nr. 20018502
(Englischer / English Text)

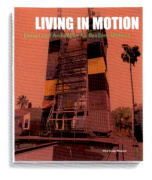

**Living in motion –
Design und Architekur
für flexibles Wohnen**

Paperback
Format 28 x 24 cm
Seiten / pages 288
mehr als 500 meist farbige
Abbildungen / over 500
mainly color illustrations
Herausgeber / Editor:
Alexander von Vegesack,
Mathias Schwartz-Clauss

ISBN 978-3-931936-34-1
Art. Nr. 20017901
(Deutscher / German Text)

**Living in Motion –
Design and Architecture
for flexible Dwelling**
ISBN 978-3-931936-35-8
Art. Nr. 20017902
(Englischer / English Text)

**Le Corbusier –
Studie über die Deutsche
Kunstgewerbebewegung**

Leineneinband mit Banderole
Format 16,5 x 20 cm
Seiten / pages 224
116 Abb. (16 Farbtafeln und
100 Duplex-Abbildungen)
116 pictures (16 color and
100 duplex-illustrations)
Herausgeber / Editor:
Mateo Kries,
Alexander von Vegesack

ISBN 978-3-931936-28-0
Art. Nr. 20018601
(Deutscher / German Text)

**Le Corbusier –
A Study of the Decorative Art
Movement in Germany**
ISBN 978-3-931936-29-7
Art. Nr. 20018602
(Englischer / English Text)

**Grow your own house –
Simón Vélez und die
Bambusarchitektur /
Grow your own house –
Simón Vélez and the bamboo
architecture**

Paperback
Format 29 x 24 cm
Seiten / pages 265
300 Abbildungen / illustrations
Herausgeber / Editor:
Alexander von Vegesack,
Mateo Kries

ISBN 978-3-931936-25-9
Art. Nr. 20016509
(Deutscher und Englischer /
German and English Text)

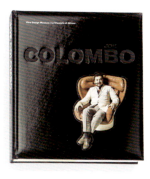

**Joe Colombo –
Die Erfindung der Zukunft**

Hardcover
Format 28 x 24 cm
Seiten / pages 304
515 Abbildungen / illustrations
Hrsg. / Editor: Alexander
von Vegesack, Mateo Kries

ISBN 978-3-931936-57-0
Art. Nr. 20018401
(Deutscher / German Text)

**Joe Colombo –
Inventing the Future**
ISBN 978-3-931936-58-7
Art. Nr. 20018402
(Englischer / English Text)

**Joe Colombo –
L'invention du futur**
ISBN 978-3-931936-73-0
Art. Nr. 20018403
(Französischer / French Text)

Vitra Design Museum Publications

Alle Publikationen des Vitra Design Museums erhalten Sie in ausgewählten Buchhandlungen oder direkt unter www.design-museum.com
All publications are available for purchase from our exclusive distributors, or ordered directly at www.design-museum.com

02/2010

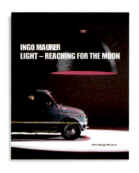

**Leben unter dem Halbmond –
Die Wohnkulturen der
arabischen Welt**

Paperback
Format 33 x 24 cm
Seiten / pages 320
mehr als 430 meist farbige
Abbildungen / over 430
mainly color illustrations
Hrsg. / Editor: Alexander
von Vegesack, Mateo Kries

**Living under the Crescent
Moon – Domestic Culture
in the Arab World**
ISBN 978-3-931936-41-9
Art. Nr. 20010402
(Englischer / English Text)

**Vivir bajo la Media Luna –
Las culturas domésticas del
mundo árabe**
ISBN 978-3-931936-45-7
Art. Nr. 20010404
(Spanischer / Spanish Text)

**100 Masterpieces aus der Sammlung
des Vitra Design Museums**

Paperpack
Format 30 x 23 cm
Seiten / pages 270
350 Abbildungen / illustrations
Hrsg. / Editor: Alexander von Vegesack,
Mathias Schwartz-Clauss, Peter Dunas

**ISBN 978-3-9804070-2-1
Art. Nr. 20010001
(Deutscher / German Text)**

**100 Masterpieces from the
Vitra Design Museum Collection**
ISBN 978-3-9804070-3-8
Art. Nr. 20010002
(Englischer / English Text)

**100 chefs-d'œuvre de la
Vitra Design Museum**
ISBN 978-3-9804070-4-5
Art. Nr. 20010003
(Französischer / French Text)

**100 Obras maestras de la
Colección del Vitra Design Museum**
ISBN 978-3-931936-63-1
Art. Nr. 20010004
(Spanischer / Spanish Text)

Verner Panton – Das Gesamtwerk

Hardcover
Format 29,5 x 23 cm
Seiten / pages 384
650 Abbildungen / illustrations
Inkl. / Includes CD-ROM
Hrsg. / Editor: Alexander
von Vegesack, Mathias Remmele

**ISBN 978-3-931936-22-8
Art. Nr. 20016301
(Deutscher / German Text)**

Verner Panton – Das Gesamtwerk

Paperback
Format 29,5 x 23 cm
Seiten / pages 384
650 Abbildungen / illustrations
Hrsg. / Editor: Alexander
von Vegesack, Mathias Remmele

**ISBN 978-3-931936-21-1
Art. Nr. 20016101
(Deutscher / German Text)**

Verner Panton – Complete Works
ISBN 978-3-931936-23-5
Art. Nr. 20016102
(Englischer / English Text)

**Ingo Maurer
Light – Reaching for the Moon**

Paperback
Format 27 x 21cm
Seiten / pages 176
ca. 100 farbige Abbildungen /
colour illustrations
Herausgeber / Editor:
Alexander von Vegesack,
Jochen Eisenbrand

**ISBN 978-3-931936-43-3
Art. Nr. 20010509
(Deutscher und Englischer /
German and English Text)**

**Marcel Breuer –
Design und Architektur**

Hardcover
Format 25,5 x 24,5 cm
Seiten / pages 320
ca. 300 Abb. / illus.
Hrsg. / Editor: Alexander
von Vegesack, Mathias Remmele

**ISBN 978-3-931936-46-4
Art. Nr. 20010301
(Deutscher / German Text)**

**Marcel Breuer –
Design and Architecture**
ISBN 978-3-931936-42-6
Art. Nr. 20010302
(Englischer / English Text)

Automobility – Was uns bewegt

Paperback
Format 29 x 20 cm
Seiten / pages 384
600 Abbildungen / illustrations
Hrsg. / Editor: Alexander
von Vegesack, Mateo Kries

**ISBN 978-3-931936-17-4
Art. Nr. 20015601
(Deutscher / German Text)**

**OPEN HOUSE – Architektur und
Technologie für intelligentes Wohnen**

Paperback
Format 22,7 x 28,7 cm
Seiten / pages 268
ca. 300 Abbildungen / pictures
Hrsg. / Editor: Alexander von
Vegesack, Jochen Eisenbrand

**ISBN 978-3-931936-65-5
Art. Nr. 20008201
(Deutscher / German Text)**

**OPEN HOUSE. Architecture and
Technology for intelligent Living**
ISBN 978-3-931936-66-2
Art. Nr. 20008202
(Englischer / English Text)

**Antibodies / Antikörper
Fernando & Humberto Campana
1989-2009**

Paperback
Format 32,5 x 24,5 cm
Seiten / pages 128
250 Abbildungen / illustrations
Herausgeber / Editor:
Alexander von Vegesack,
Mathias Schwartz-Clauss

**ISBN 978-3-931936-47-1
Art. Nr. 20080301
(Deutscher und Englischer /
German and English Text)**

www.design-museum.com

Vitra Design Museum, Charles-Eames-Str. 1, D-79576 Weil am Rhein, Tel. +49 (0)7621-702 3718, Fax +49 (0)7621-702 4718, verlag@design-museum.com

62

63

64

45

66

47

67

68

69

70

INSPIRATION /
INSPIRATION

71

73

74

75

LOGISTIK /
LOGISTICS

77

76

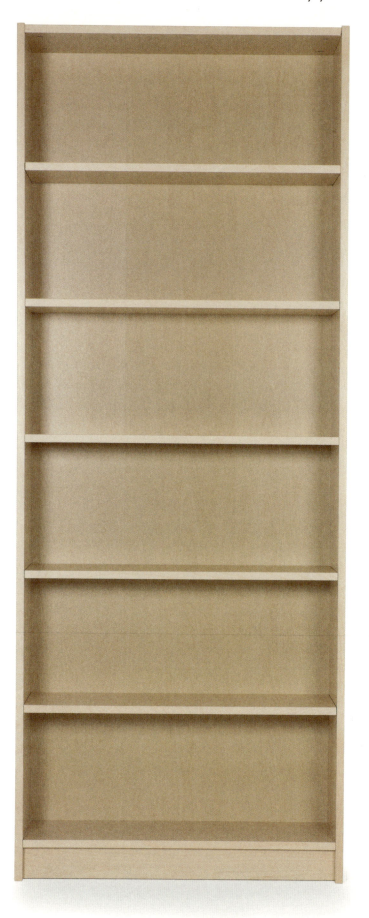

78

79

56
Charles & Ray Eames
Schweißvorrichtung für einen 3-teiligen Aluminiumstuhl,
Experiment / mold for welding the three-piece
aluminium chair, experiment
1948
Eames Office, Venice, CA
45 x 52 x 51,5 cm
Gips / plaster
Collection Vitra Design Museum, Weil am Rhein

57
Charles & Ray Eames
Teile des 3-teiligen Aluminiumstuhls, Experiment /
parts of the three-piece aluminium chair, experiment
1948
Eames Office, Venice, CA
52 x 50 x 50,5 cm (montiert / mounted)
gestanztes Aluminiumblech / stamped sheet aluminum
Collection Vitra Design Museum, Weil am Rhein

Nachdem sich Versuche, einen ungepolsterten, aber
bequemen Schalensitz nur aus Sperrholz zu formen, als
unpraktikabel erwiesen hatten, setzte das Eames Office
die Experimente mit Schalen aus Aluminiumblechen fort,
die unter hohem Druck in Form geprägt und dann zusam-
mengeschweißt wurden. Damaligen Berechnungen zufolge
hätte mit diesem Verfahren ein Stuhl ohne Armlehnen
für nur 5,80 $ produziert werden können. Zur Serienpro-
duktion kam es jedoch nicht, da man zwischenzeitlich
die Vorteile einer Fabrikation aus Fiberglas erkannt hatte.

After attempts to create a non-upholstered but comfortable seat shell entirely out of plywood proved impracticable,
the Eames Office continued its experimentations with
shells made from sheets of aluminium that were stamped
into shape under high pressure and then welded together.
According to calculations at the time, this technique could
have produced a chair without armrests for just $5.80.
It never reached the stage of mass production, however,
due to the intervening discovery of the superior qualities
of fibreglass.

58
Charles & Ray Eames
Stuhlsitzschale (S-Typ), Arbeitsexemplar zur Einstellung
der Shockmounts / chair shell (S-type), working model
for the adjustment of shock mounts
ca. 1952
Eames Office, Venice, CA
44,2 x 48 x 50,5 cm
Fiberglas; Gummi / fibreglass; rubber
Collection Vitra Design Museum, Weil am Rhein

59
Charles & Ray Eames
Stuhlsitzschale (S-Typ), Entwicklungsstufe zur Form-
gebung / chair shell (S-type), development stage of
shape design
ca. 1952
Eames Office, Venice, CA
42 x 48,5 x 50,5 cm
Fiberglas
Collection Vitra Design Museum, Weil am Rhein

60
Charles & Ray Eames
Stuhlsitzschale (S-Typ) / chair shell (S-type)
1948–52
Herman Miller Furniture Co., Zeeland, MI/ Vitra AG, Basel
43 x 47,5 x 53 cm
Fiberglas / fiberglass
Collection Vitra Design Museum, Weil am Rhein

61
Heinz Witthoeft
Armsessel / armchair
Tail 13
1967
65 x 65 x 65 cm
thermoplastisch verformter Kunststoff /
deformed thermoplastic
Bernhard Schweyer, Fellbach

In zahlreichen Varianten lotete der Designer und Künstler
Heinz Witthoeft das gestalterische und funktionale
Potential geometrischer Grundformen aus. Der Entwurf
für den *Tail 13* wurde jedoch trotz seiner formal wie tech-
nisch einleuchtenden Effizienz nie in Serie produziert –
bis auf sechs Sessel für das dänische Fernsehen. So steht
das Objekt sowohl mit seiner Entstehungsgeschichte
wie auch als Figur für den Moment des Übergangs von der
Idee zum Gebrauchsgegenstand.

In numerous variants, the work of designer and artist
Heinz Witthoeft was oriented towards probing the
aesthetic and functional potential of basic geometric
shapes. Despite its formally and technically convincing
efficiency, his design for *Tail 13* never went into serial
production—except for six armchairs made for Danish
television. Thus, it stands, together with the history of its
origin, as a figure symbolizing the moment of transition
from idea to product.

62
Gerald Summers
Stuhl / chair
ca. 1938
Makers of Simple Furniture, Ltd., London
74,6 x 56,4 x 58 cm
gebogenes Sperrholz, lackiert / bent plywood, lacquered
Collection Vitra Design Museum, Weil am Rhein

Mit geringem Materialverlust aus nur einem Stück Sperrholz geschnitten und gebogen, erfüllt diese verblüffend
einfache Konstruktion alle Anforderungen an einen
bequemen und preiswerten Stapelstuhl, der zudem die
damals populäre Stromlinienform aufnimmt. Die Tücken
liegen jedoch in der Nutzung: Das Möbel ist relativ
schwer, lässt sich schlecht greifen, und die Stabilität der
Hinterbeine sollte man nicht herausfordern.

Cut and bent from a single piece of plywood with minimal
loss of material, this astonishingly simple construction
fulfils all the requirements of a comfortable and inexpensive stackable chair while incorporating the popular
streamlined contours of the era. The pitfalls lie in its actual
use: it is relatively heavy and difficult to grasp and the
stability of the rear legs should not be too severely tested.

63
Shiro Kuramata
Bodenlampe / floor lamp
Oba-Q
1972
Ishimaru Co., Ltd., Tokyo
56,5 x 66 x 66 cm
Plexiglas / plexiglass
Collection Vitra Design Museum, Weil am Rhein

64
Gaetano Pesce
Stuhl / chair
Golgotha
1972–73
Bracciodiferro srl, Genova
75,5 x 47 x 58 cm
Fiberglas; Polyesterharz / fiberglass; polyester resin
Collection Vitra Design Museum, Weil am Rhein

Während des Aushärtens wurden hier über zwei Leinen
gelegte, mit Polyesterharz getränkte Matten aus weißem
Fiberglasgewebe und einer Füllung aus PET-Fasern
mit den Abgüssen unterschiedlicher Gesäße in Form
gebracht. Als überzeugter Industriedesigner ist Gaetano
Pesce stets am Potential neuer Materialien und Verfahren
interessiert, wobei sein Werk zwischen Design und Kunst

changiert. Indem er das Individuum in serielle und industrielle Herstellungsprozesse integriert, verleiht er den
Gegenständen Einzigartigkeit und dem Umgang mit ihnen
eine tiefere Bedeutung.

During the hardening process of this chair by Gaetano
Pesce, resin-soaked white fibreglass cloth mats with
Dacron fibrefill were draped over two cords and shaped
with the castings of various backsides. As a committed
industrial designer, Pesce exhibits constant interest in the
potential of new materials and techniques, with an oeuvre
oscillating between design and art. By integrating the
one-off piece into serial and industrial manufacturing
processes, he lends the objects he designs a unique
character and gives deeper meaning to our interactions
with them.

65
Willy Guhl
Gartensessel / garden easy chair
1954
Eternit AG, Niederurnen
53 x 55 x 88,5 cm
Faserzement, oberflächenversiegelt / fiber cement,
surface sealed
Collection Vitra Design Museum, Weil am Rhein

Zeitgleich mit den Eames' hatte Willy Guhl an der Entwicklung eines Kunststoffschalenstuhls gearbeitet und
wie sie 1948 am „Low-cost Furniture"-Wettbewerb des
Museum of Modern Art in New York teilgenommen. Für
sein schlichtes, seriell produziertes Gartenmöbel nutzte
er die Bruch- und Zugfestigkeit von Faserbetonplatten,
wie sie für den Hausbau hergestellt wurden. Die Ab-
wicklung des Sessels entspricht genau den Maßen der
Betonplatten, die frisch gepresst in die gewünschte
Form gelegt und dann getrocknet wurden.

Parallel to the Eameses, Willy Guhl had also been
developing a chair with a plastic seat shell and likewise
took part in the 1948 "Low-Cost Furniture" competition
sponsored by the Museum of Modern Art in New York.
For his simple mass-produced garden furniture, he
utilized the tensile and breaking strength of fibre-rein-
forced concrete slabs, as manufactured for applications
in housing construction. The shape of the chair is based
on the dimensions of the concrete slabs, which are
moulded into the desired form while still wet and then
dried.

66
Maarten Van Severen
Sessel / lounge chair
Low Chair Aluminium
1993–95
Maarten Van Severen, Gent
52 x 49,5 x 93 cm
Aluminium; Gummi / aluminium; rubber
Collection Vitra Design Museum, Weil am Rhein

Technische Präzision und künstlerische Individualität
vereinen und sublimieren sich in Maarten Van Severens
Arbeiten auf einzigartige Weise. Kein Radius der Kurven
und keine Länge der Ebenen sind hier gleich; jedes Detail
ist aus einer gründlichen Kenntnis der Materialeigenschaften und mit scharfem Augenmaß genau auf die be-
queme Lagerung des menschlichen Körpers im Raum
ausgerichtet. Zwei Gummipuffer unter der rückwärtigen
Schlaufe dosieren die Schwingung beim Sitzen.

Technical precision and artistic individuality are united
and sublimated in Maarten van Severen's works in inimi-
table fashion. No two curves have the same radius, no
two planes the same length. Every detail is based on a
thorough knowledge of the material's properties and is
precisely oriented with a keen sense of proportion to
the comfortable positioning of the human body in space.
Two rubber buffers beneath the rear loop ensure gentle
movement for the sitter.

67
Ross Lovegrove
Armsessel /armchair
Air One
2000
Edra, Perignano (PI)
51 x 114 x 112,5 cm

Polyurethanschaum / polyurethane foam
Collection Vitra Design Museum, Weil am Rhein

Ross Lovegrove beschreibt sein Design als einen „organischen Essentialismus" – die Suche nach ästhetisch und ökologisch stringenten Lösungen in organischen Formen. Dieser 530 g leichte, preiswerte und gut zu recycelnde Sessel aus durchgefärbtem Schaumstoff entsteht in nur einem maschinellen Arbeitsgang.

Ross Lovegrove describes his design as "organic essentialism"—the quest for aesthetically and ecologically stringent solutions in organic forms. Weighing in at just 530 grams, this affordable and easily recycled armchair made of batch-dyed foam is produced in a single mechanized work step.

68

Architekturbüro Helmut Bätzner (H. & A. Bätzner, F. Bös)
Stapelstuhl / stacking chair
BA 1171 (Bofinger-Stuhl)
1964–65
Menzolit-Werke, Kraichtal-Menzingen, für /
for Wilhelm Bofinger KG, Ilsfeld
75 x 50,5 x 52,7 cm
durchgefärbtes, glasfaserverstärktes Polyesterharz /
integrally coloured, glass-reinfirced polyester resin
Collection Vitra Design Museum, Weil am Rhein

Dieser erste seriell hergestellte, einteilige Kunststoffstuhl der Möbelgeschichte entstand ursprünglich als leichter, witterungsbeständiger Stapelstuhl für das Staatstheater Karlsruhe. Über 20 Jahre lang wurde er mehr als 120 000 Mal produziert und mit seinen charakteristischen Beinen, die mit wenig Material hohe Stabilität gewährleisten, zum Vorbild der heute allgegenwärtigen Monoblock-Varianten.

The first plastic chair in furniture history to be mass-produced in one piece, it was originally created as a light-weight and weather-resistant chair for the Baden State Theatre in Karlsruhe. Over the course of two decades, more than 120,000 units were manufactured and, with its characteristic legs providing a high degree of stability with just a small amount of material, it serves as a model for today's omnipresent monobloc variants.

69

Jasper Morrison
Stapelstuhl / stacking chair
Air-Chair
1999
Magis srl, Motta di Livenza, TV
76,3 x 49,5 x 52,5 cm
Polypropylen / polypropylene
Collection Vitra Design Museum, Weil am Rhein

Dieser Stapelstuhl ist das Ergebnis eines relativ unkomplizierten Entwurfsprozesses, aber einer sehr aufwändigen Entwicklung des Formwerkzeugs für die Serienproduktion. Nach dem Verfahren eines Spritzgusses mit Gasinjektion entsteht der komplette Stuhl mit seinen unterschiedlichen Dicken und Hohlräumen in einem einzigen maschinellen Arbeitsgang.

In contrast to the time-consuming procedure of developing a mould for mass production, this stackable chair is the result of a relatively uncomplicated design process. The technique of gas-assisted injection moulding forms the complete chair, with its different thicknesses and cavities, in a single mechanical work step.

70

Stephan Schulz
Schale / bowl
2006
Studio Stephan Schulz, Halle a.d. Saale
16,5 x 35 x 35 cm
Beton, gegossen / cast concrete
Collection Martin Hartung

Ungeachtet der robusten Materialeigenschaften zeigt sich an der filigranen, aber sehr stabilen Schale, welche Ruhe dieser Werkstoff ausstrahlen kann. Das schlichte Objekt scheint seinem Gewicht zu trotzen und leicht über dem Boden zu schweben.

In spite of its robust physical properties, this delicate—

looking yet highly stable bowl demonstrates the calm that its material is able to exude. The simple object seems to defy its weight and float ever so slightly above the surface on which it rests.

INSPIRATION / INSPIRATION

71

Frank Gehry
Stuhl / chair
Side Chair (Prototyp / prototype)
1972
Easy Edges Inc., New York, NY
82,4 x 36,4 x 54,8 cm
Wellkarton; Hartfaser-Platte; Holz /
corrugated cardboard; hardboard; wood
Collection Vitra Design Museum, Weil am Rhein

48 Lagen Wellpappe mit einer Schablone ausgeschnitten, verklebt, zur Stabilisierung mit drei Rundhölzern durchbohrt und die Außenseiten mit ausgesägten Hartfaserplatten verstärkt. Nach dieser Do-it-yourself-Methode entstand eine ganze Möbelserie, die Gehry in Anspielung auf die ebenso schablonenhafte Hard-Edge-Malerei seiner Zeit Easy Edges nannte.

Forty-eight layers of corrugated cardboard are cut out with a template, glued, bored through with three wooden dowels for stability and reinforced on the outer edges with sawn-out pieces of hardboard. This do-it-yourself method was applied to create an entire furniture series, which Gehry named Easy Edges in allusion to the similarly template-like Hard Edge painting from that time.

72

Rody Graumans
Deckenlampe / ceiling lamp
DMD 08, 85 Lamps
1993
Droog Design, Amsterdam
100 x 70 x 70 cm
Glühbirnen; Fassungen; Kabel; Kabelbinder /
light bulbs; cabeling; mounts; cable connectors
Collection Vitra Design Museum, Weil am Rhein

73

Stiletto (Frank Schreiner)
Armstuhl / armchair
Consumer's Rest
1983
Stiletto Studios, Berlin
94,5 x 71,7 x 76 cm
lackierter Stahl; Kunststoff / lacquered steel; plastic
Collection Vitra Design Museum, Weil am Rhein

Ironisch schrieb Stiletto über seine eigenen Möbel, sie „sollen klar sein im Aufbau, industriell reell, funktionsgerecht Längemalbreitemalwirbelsäule, stabil und solide, serienproduziert [...] Redesign hat hier weniger mit Recycling, mehr mit Rebirthing zu tun". Ausgerüstet mit einem Schweißgerät, einem PVC-Lappen und einer Sprühdose, entlarvt der (Wieder-)Geburtshelfer die Vereinnahmung durch den Konsumterror und den Schein von Design.

With intentional irony, Stiletto wrote about his own furniture that it "should be clearly constructed, industrially real, functionally length-times-width-times-spine, stable and solid, mass-produced... Redesign has less to do with recycling here, more to do with rebirthing". Equipped with a welding set, PVC cloth, and spray can, the (re)birth attendant exposes the appropriation of an oppressive consumerism and a semblance of design.

74

Achille & Pier Giacomo Castiglioni
Hocker / stool
No. 220 (Mezzadro)
1954–57
Zanotta spa, Nova Milanese, MI
52 x 49 x 53,5 cm
verchromter Stahl; lackiertes Stahlblech; Buche /
chromed steel; lacquered sheet steel; beech
Collection Vitra Design Museum, Weil am Rhein

In diesem ästhetischen Manifest wurden bereits industriell hergestellte Gegenstände wie ein ergonomischer Traktorsitz und ein federnder Bandstahl, die den Anforderungen ihrer Funktionen optimal entsprechen, miteinander kombiniert. Verbindungen sind jedoch stets kritische Stellen, an denen sich die Belastungen unterschiedlich auswirken und wechselseitig potenzieren. Den Castiglioni-Brüdern wird dies bewusst gewesen sein, weshalb der *Mezzadro* erst 1970, als Designikone jeder Kritik enthoben, in Produktion ging.

This aesthetic manifesto joins together pre-manufactured industrial objects such as an ergonomic tractor seat and a strip of spring steel, each optimally fulfilling its individual functional requirements. Combinations, however, always represent critical junctures at which different pressures exert varying impact and intensify one another. Aware of this, the Castiglioni Brothers held off on producing the *Mezzadro* until 1970, by which time it was already an established design icon and beyond criticism.

75

Enzo Mari
Stuhl / chair
Proposta per un'autoprogettazione
1973
Enzo Mari, Milano
85,5 x 50 x 53 cm
Holz / wood
Collection Vitra Design Museum, Weil am Rhein

Der Stuhl ist Teil einer kompletten Möbelserie aus Tischen, Betten, Sitz- und Aufbewahrungsmöbeln, die aus rohen Holzbrettern, Schrauben und Muttern auf unterschiedliche Weise zusammengebaut werden können. Das mit dem Prinzip des modularen Systemmöbels verwandte Konzept war als Provokation des kommerziellen Establishments und Appell an die autonome Kreativität des Verbrauchers gedacht.

This chair is part of a complete furniture series consisting of tables, beds, seats, and storage furniture that can be variously assembled from unfinished wooden boards, nuts, and bolts. Akin to the principle of the modular furniture system, the concept was intended to provoke the commercial establishment and appeal to the autonomous creativity of the user.

LOGISTIK / LOGISTICS

76

BILLY (Karton-Verpackung / cardboard packaging)
undatiert / undated
Ikea, Älmhult
12,5 x 28,7 x 203 cm
Pappe / cardboard
Collection Vitra Design Museum, Weil am Rhein

77

Gilles Lundgren
Regal / shelf
BILLY
1978
Ikea, Älmhult
202 x 80 x 28 cm
Holz, furniert / wood, veneered
Collection Vitra Design Museum, Weil am Rhein

Gillis Lundgren begann 1953 als vierter Mitarbeiter bei IKEA und führte dort, ursprünglich um Versandkosten zu sparen, den Verkauf von Möbeln als Bausätze ein. Voraussetzung für dieses Prinzip ist der einfache, von klaren Anleitungen unterstützte Aufbau. Das über 40 Millionen Mal verkaufte *Billy*-Regalsystem wird in Teilen verschiedener Größe und Farbe angeboten, die man miteinander verbinden und durch Zusatzelemente wie Türen ergänzen kann.

Hired as IKEA's fourth employee in 1953, Gillis Lundgren introduced the sale of furniture in self-assembly kits, originally to save on shipping costs. A necessary pre-requisite for this principle is a simple design paired with clear instructions. With over 40 million units sold, the *Billy* shelving system is offered in components of varying size and colour, which can be combined as desired and supplemented with additional elements such as cabinet doors.

78

Gebr. Thonet
Demonstrationsmodell im Maßstab 1:1 / demonstration
model in a 1:1 scale
Transportkiste von 1 m³ mit 36 zerlegten Stühlen *Nr. 14* /
one-cubic-metre transport crate with 36 disassembled
No. 14 chairs
1986
97 x 87 x 105 cm
Bugholz; Plexiglas / bent wood; plexiglass
Collection Alexander von Vegesack, Lessac-Confolens

36 Exemplare des in seine wenigen Einzelteile zerlegten
Stuhles *Nr. 14* konnten in 1 m³ großen Kisten weltweit
an Thonets Vertretungen in den Geschäftszentren der
Metropolen versandt werden.

Disassembled into their few parts, three dozen of the
No. 14 chairs can be packed into a single one-cubic-
metrecrate and shipped to Thonet's sales offices in
metropolitan business centres around the world.

79

Michael Thonet & Söhne
Stuhl / chair
Nr. 14 / No. 14
1859–60
Gebr. Thonet, Wien
92,5 x 42,5 x 50 cm
gebogenes Buchenholz; Rohrgeflecht / bent beech wood;
cane work
Collection Vitra Design Museum, Weil am Rhein

Dieses erfolgreichste Produkt der Möbelgeschichte ist
das Ergebnis eines komplexen technischen Entwicklungsprozesses, der von den Qualitäten des Rohstoffs (der
Biegsamkeit und Stabilität von Buchenholz) ausging
und den auf viele Millionen Stühle umzurechnenden Aufwand für die Produktion, die auch heute noch weitgehend
manuell erfolgt, konsequent reduzierte.

The most successful product in furniture history, this
design is the result of a complex technical development
process, beginning with the qualities of the raw material
(the pliability and stability of beechwood) and ending
with the distribution of millions of chairs while systemi-
cally reducing the cost of production, which is still largely
performed by hand.

Für ein Treppenhaus im Gebäude des Vitra Design Museums
wurde eine Klanginstallation des Künstlers Hubert
Steins realisiert / For a staircase in the Vitra Design Museum
building, a sound installation was realized by the artist
Hubert Steins:

Hubert Steins
zufallsgesteuerte Klanginstallation achtkanalig /
random-generated eight-channel sound installation
Klangröhre(n)
2000/2010
(Format und Ausführung variabel /
variable format and execution)
Tonträger, Audiotechnik, 8 Lautsprecher /
audio recordings and equipment, eight speakers
im Besitz des Künstlers / courtesy of the artist

Wiebke Lang

HELDEN DES ALLTAGS – VOM UMGANG MIT DINGEN IM DIGITALEN ZEITALTER /
HEROES OF THE EVERYDAY – DEALING WITH THINGS IN THE DIGITAL AGE

Alfred Neweczerzal,
Sparschäler, *Rex*, 1947.
→ Abb. 45, S. 21

Alfred Neweczerzal,
peeler, *Rex*, 1947.
→ ill. 45, p. 21

Das anonyme Design einer Heftzwecke oder eines Maßbandes bedeutet für den Benutzer vertraute Handhabung und bietet mit seiner unaufdringlich reduzierten Erscheinung eine erholsame Abwechslung in einer Produktwelt, in der die lautstarke Rhetorik semantisch aufgeladener Objekte dominiert – wie bei computergenerierten Möbeln oder provozierenden Produktkonzepten zwischen Kunst und Design. Wohl auch deshalb manifestiert sich seit einiger Zeit ein allgemeines Interesse an Alltagsdingen wie Büroklammern, Wasserflaschen und Post-its. 1976 etwa fand auf der Mathildenhöhe in Darmstadt die Ausstellung „Die gewöhnlichen Dinge" statt, 1995 sogar „World Stuff – Die gewöhnlichsten Dinge der Welt" in der Rotterdamer Kunsthalle. Im ersten Jahrzehnt des neuen Jahrtausends waren gleich mehrere Präsentationen kleiner Objekte zu sehen: „Humble Masterpieces" im Museum of Modern Art in New York, „Under a Tenner" im Design Museum London, „Every Thing Design" im Museum für Gestaltung Zürich und „Super Normal – Sensations of the Ordinary" mit archetypischen Alltagsgegenständen in Tokio, London, Mailand und Berlin; in Berlin ist ihnen sogar ein ganzes Museum gewidmet – das „Museum der Dinge".

Die meisten dieser Dinge überzeugen weniger durch ihre gute Form als vielmehr durch ihre schlichte, verständliche Gestalt und ihre Praktikabilität. In einer sich stetig wandelnden Produktwelt erscheint die Tatsache beinah revolutionär, dass viele der bescheidenen Alltagsprodukte gar keinen Anlass zur Veränderung liefern, weil sich ihre Funktionstüchtigkeit und ihr adäquates Äußeres bewährt haben und kaum optimieren lassen: Immer wieder verblüffend gut funktioniert etwa der Schweizer Sparschäler *Rex*, der von Alfred Neweczerzal bereits 1947 erfunden und im selben Jahr patentiert wurde. Seinem U-förmigen Bügel, der beweglichen, scharfen Schneide und dem Abstandshalter, der ein zu tiefes Abschälen von Apfel- oder Kartoffelschalen verhindert, ist nichts hinzuzufügen. Ähnlich fundamental sind Form und Funktionalität der Reißzwecke, deren Erfindung Johann Kirsten, einem Uhrmacher aus der Uckermark, um 1902 zugeschrieben wird.

Die Anonymität dieser banalen, aber unverzichtbaren Dinge wirkt heute, da Designer wie Filmstars gefeiert werden, nachgerade sympathisch. Diese unprätentiösen Objekte scheinen eine personalisierte Autorenschaft gar nicht nötig zu haben – sie überzeugen durch ihre unaufdringliche Unterstützung menschlicher Alltagshandlungen. Genau diese Nähe zu unseren Bedürfnissen ist es, die in einer sich rasant wandelnden Gesellschaft für Aufmerksamkeit sorgt.

Denn die Bedürfnisse des Menschen bleiben die gleichen. Betrachten wir einmal das Streben nach Mobilität, das sich seit der Erfindung des Rades stetig steigert und nach immer mehr Tempo und Komplexität verlangt und besonders in einer globalisierten Welt an Bedeutung gewinnt. Dass zahlreiche simple Alltagsdinge diesen Wunsch nach Mobilität bedienen, demonstriert

----

The anonymous design of a drawing pin, light bulb, or tape measure implies familiar operation and handling for the user as well as an unassuming and minimal appearance. Thus, it constitutes a refreshing alternative in a world of products dominated by the loud rhetoric of semantically loaded objects, be they computer-generated furniture pieces or provocative product concepts at the intersection of art and design. This circumstance has aroused for some time now a general interest in the things of everyday life, such as paper clips, water bottles, and Post-its. In 1976, for instance, the Mathildenhöhe Institute in Darmstadt hosted an exhibition entitled "The Ordinary Things", while in 1995 the exhibition "World Stuff: The Most Ordinary Things in the World" was held at Kunsthal Rotterdam. The first decade of the new millennium saw an intensification of interest in the topic, with multiple exhibitions of everyday objects held all over the world: "Humble Masterpieces" at the Museum of Modern Art in New York, "Under a Tenner" at the Design Museum London, "Every Thing Design" at the Museum of Design Zurich, and "Super Normal: Sensations of the Ordinary", which presented archetypal objects of daily life and was exhibited in Tokyo, London, Milan and Berlin. In Berlin there is even a museum dedicated entirely to the subject—the Museum of Things.

What distinguishes most of these "things" is not so much their good form as their simple, easy-to-understand shape and practicability. Amidst a constantly changing world of commodities, it seems almost revolutionary that so many of these humble, everyday products give no cause for change because their adequate functionality and appearance have proven sufficient and therefore resist further optimization. The Swiss vegetable peeler *Rex*, for example, which was invented and patented by Alfred Neweczerzal already in 1947, continues to perform astoundingly well. The U-shaped handle, the sharp flexible blade, and the spacer that prevents the user from cutting too deeply into an apple or potato make it hard to improve upon. Similarly fundamental are the form and functionality of the drawing pin, whose invention in 1902 is ascribed to Johann Kirsten, a watchmaker in Uckermark, Germany.

In an age when designers have achieved movie-star status, there is something almost charming about the anonymity of these banal yet indispensable objects. Due to their unpretentious nature, they seem exempt from the need for personalized authorship, their compelling character stemming from the unobtrusive support they afford everyday human activities. In a society marked by rapid change, it is precisely this close fit with our basic needs that makes them stand out.

seine Signifikanz: Die Babyflasche, die die Mutterbrust bei Abwesenheit ersetzt, ermöglicht dem Kind eine zeit- und ortsunabhängige Nahrungsaufnahme. Das multifunktionale Gummiband hält beliebige Dinge zusammen, stabilisiert sie und macht sie transportabel. Die Batterie liefert fern der Steckdose Strom, und der iPod macht Musik mobil.

Die Königsdisziplin des effizienten Mobilmachens ist das *packaging design*, dessen Ziel es ist, Dinge mit minimalem Material- und Kostenaufwand möglichst effektiv zu transportieren, zu schützen, zu lagern und zu stapeln. Ein Eierkarton, der seinen fragilen Inhalt trotz seiner leichten, niederkomplexen Pappform sicher transportier- und stapelbar macht und ihn zudem dekorativ präsentiert, lässt sich nur schwer optimieren. Maximale Funktionalität bietet auch die transparente, ringförmige Folie mit runden Ausstanzungen, die Getränkeflaschen oder -dosen zusammenhält und transportabel macht: Ihre Essenz besteht in der Negativform, dem Loch. So wird, unter dem Aspekt der Nachhaltigkeit, die Müllproduktion verringert, während gleichzeitig das Produkt in den Vordergrund tritt. Verpackungen sind immer Diener des Produktes, das sie umschließen, und des Anwenders, der sie nutzt. Je selbstverständlicher und komfortabler ein Produkt menschliche Bedürfnisse befriedigt, desto größer ist die Chance, dass es von einer Gesellschaft langfristig internalisiert wird.

Der Medientheoretiker Marshall McLuhan ging so weit zu behaupten, dass Instrumente und Maschinen als erweiterte Gliedmaßen selbst Teil des menschlichen Körpers werden.[1] Dabei beschleunigen und verstärken sie, von der Schere über die Glühbirne bis zum Telefon, alltägliche Prozesse. Aktuelle Beispiele demonstrieren, wie stark diese Werkzeuge Geschwindigkeit, Maßstäbe und Formen des menschlichen Handelns und der Kommunikation modifizieren: Die Demokratisierung von Information durch das Web 2.0 etwa hat die Werte unserer Gesellschaft, das Verhältnis zu den Medien nachhaltig verändert. Und indem das Internet mit Notebooks und Smartphones immer mobiler und, ständig verfügbar, zunehmend in den Alltag implementiert wird, forcieren die Geräte einen nie abbrechenden Informationsfluss.

Die Auseinandersetzung mit banalen Alltagshelfern verweist also nicht allein auf grundlegende Produkt-, sondern auch auf menschliche Handlungsformen und liefert damit Denkanstöße für Interaktion in einer digitalen Welt, die keine lange Tradition und wenig Vorbilder hat. Mittlerweile ist die erste Generation der *digital natives*, also der Menschen, die ein Leben ohne Handy und Internet nicht mehr kennen, erwachsen geworden. Ihr soziales Leben findet längst zu großen Teilen in einer virtuellen Welt statt; digitale Netzwerke wie Facebook und Musikabspielgeräte wie der iPod sind heute kaum weniger alltäglich als die Milchkartons in der Küche. Seit Computerchips anstelle von Mechanik zum Einsatz kommen, sagt die äußere Form eines Produktes nicht mehr viel über seine Funktion und Bedienbarkeit aus. Während sich analoge Alltagsdinge über Generationen hinweg ent-

----

The crux of the matter is that, ultimately, human needs remain the same. Let us consider the quest for mobility, which has grown steadily since the invention of the wheel, demanding ever-greater speed and complexity and increasingly gaining in importance, especially in today's globalized world. The fact that such a large number of simple, everyday objects satisfy this desire for mobility attests to its significance. The baby bottle substitutes for the mother's breast in periods of absence and allows the child to obtain nourishment independent of place and time. The multifunctional rubber band holds together all manner of things, stabilizes them, and makes them transportable. The battery supplies power away from power sockets and the iPod lets people listen to music on the go.

The epitome of efficient mobilization is packaging design, with its aim of transporting, protecting, storing, and stacking different objects as effectively as possible and at a minimal expense of materials and costs. Despite its simple, lightweight cardboard form, it would be difficult to find a better solution than the egg carton for securely transporting and stacking its fragile contents, while at the same time presenting them in an aesthetically appealing fashion. Maximum functionality is also achieved by the transparent, ring-shaped plastic film, with round cut-outs, that holds together beverage cans and makes them portable. Its essence consists in the negative form, the hole. In terms of sustainability, the creation of waste is thereby decreased, while the product itself is brought to the fore. In other words, packaging is always the servant of the product it encloses and those who make use of it; and the more intuitively and comfortably a product satisfies human needs, the greater the chance it will be internalized by society in the long run.

The media theorist Marshall McLuhan went so far as to assert that tools and machines have themselves become part of the human body, extended limbs of sorts.[1] From scissors and light bulbs up to the telephone, they accelerate and reinforce everyday processes. Current examples demonstrate the degree to which these tools modify the speed, scale, and forms of human actions and communication. The democratization of information through Web 2.0 applications, for instance, has permanently changed the values of our society and our relationship to the media. And as the internet becomes increasingly mobile with the help of laptops and smartphones and more deeply implemented in daily life through its nonstop availability, these devices are accelerating the neverceasing flow of information.

The investigation of these banal, everyday "prostheses" hence not only refers to basic forms of products but also

wickeln und durchsetzen konnten, müssen die Ansprüche an die neuerdings genauso alltäglichen Mensch-Maschine-Interaktionen neu definiert und adäquate Gesten erst gefunden werden, um sie ebenso selbstverständlich in den Alltag einzufügen wie Schere, Büroklammer und Sparschäler.

Wie Erfolg versprechend es sein kann, sich bei der Entwicklung digitaler Produkte von der sinnlichen Alltagswelt inspirieren zu lassen, demonstrieren Apple-Kassenschlager wie iPod und iPhone, deren Touchscreens mit intuitiv verständlichen Ges-ten, abgeleitet von Bewegungsabläufen im realen Leben, bedient werden. Mit der freundlich-reduzierten Produktsemantik der Apparate und der selbstverständlich-haptischen Bedienbarkeit ihrer Benutzeroberflächen holt Apple die sinnliche Dimension in die digitale Welt zurück – und schafft mit dieser Schein-Einfachheit Vertrauen beim Konsumenten. Denn Komplexität sorgt für Verunsicherung: Wäre das Interface der Suchmaschine Google nicht so einfach aufgebaut, würde der User an der Vielzahl von Funktionen und Optionen schnell verzweifeln. *Simplexity* lautet das Kunstwort, das diese Verbindung von Komplexität in der Tiefe mit Einfachheit an der Oberfläche beschreibt.

John Maeda, amerikanischer Medienkünstler und Kommunikationsdesigner, setzt sich in seinem Buch *The Laws of Simplicity*[2] mit der Vereinfachung verdichteter Information auseinander und artikuliert dafür zehn Gesetze: In den ersten beiden plädiert er für *Reduktion*, also durchdachtes Weglassen, und *Organisation*, also

Übersichtlichkeit durch klare Strukturen – altbekannte Grundlagen für jeden Designer. Neue Perspektiven liefern das achte Gesetz, Vertrauen: „Vertrauen auf die Einfachheit", und das zehnte Gesetz, *Das Eine*: „Einfachheit bedeutet, das Offensichtliche zu entfernen und das Sinnvolle hinzuzufügen." Während das „Offensichtliche" eines Sparschälers – der Griff, die Schneide und der Abstandhalter – gleichzeitig auch das „Sinnvolle" ist, ist es kaum möglich, alle Funktionen digitaler Produkte an der Benutzeroberfläche darzustellen. Digitale Technik lässt sich kaum mehr nachvollziehen, wir müssen ihren einfachen Oberflächen zwangs-läufig vertrauen.

Analoge Alltagsgegenstände haben aufgrund ihrer durchgängigen Simplizität den digitalen offensichtlich eine fundamentale Qualität voraus, und zwar ihre Potenzialität auf der funktionalen und der semantischen Ebene. Das zeigt sich beispielsweise an der rund um den Globus benutzten Plastik-Wasserflasche: Die PET-Wasserflasche erhält mit der SODIS-Methode, dem „Solar Water Disinfection"-Prinzip, eine einschneidend neue Funktion, insofern als sie sich in Drittwelt-Ländern zum Desinfizieren des Trinkwassers einsetzen lässt: In Wasser, das abgefüllt in PET-Flaschen mindestens sechs Stunden in der Sonne gelegen hat, sterben die Durchfall erregenden Keime zuverlässig ab.

Nicht auf der funktionalen, sondern auf einer semantischen Ebene wiederum erfuhr die Büroklammer einen existenziellen Wandel: Nachdem Johan Vaaler, norwegischer Physiker und Mit-

----

to fundamental patterns of human action, thus providing food for thought regarding the nature of interaction in a digital world with neither a long tradition nor many role models. Meanwhile, the first generation of digital natives— that is, people who have never known life without cell phones and the internet —has come of age. The majority of their social life has long been transported into a virtual world, with digital networks like Facebook and portable music players like the iPod hardly less ordinary these days than the milk carton in the kitchen. Ever since computer chips began to replace mechanical systems, the exterior form of a product no longer says much about its function and operability. Whereas analogue objects of daily life developed and established themselves over generations, the demands placed on the equally commonplace man-machine interactions of today have to be defined anew and adequate gestures must first be

found in order for them to become integrated into daily life as naturally as scissors, paper clips, and vegetable peelers.

The potential success of drawing inspiration from the everyday world of the senses in order to develop digital products is demonstrated by such Apple blockbusters as the iPod and iPhone, whose touchscreens are operated with intuitively comprehensible gestures derived from real-life motion sequences. With the minimal yet friendly product semantics of these devices and the straightforward haptic operability of their user interfaces, Apple brings the sensory dimension back into the digital world while building trust with consumers through the seeming simplicity of its products. For complexity creates uncertainty. If the interface of the Google search engine, for example, were not so simply structured, the user would quickly become overwhelmed by the multitude of functions and options.

Thus, the term "simplexity" was aptly coined in order to describe the complexity that underlies such simplicity.

In his book *The Laws of Simplicity*,[2] the American media artist and communication designer John Maeda probes the simplification of complex information and puts forth ten laws. The first two are Reduce, referring to thoughtful omission, and Organize, meaning comprehensibility through clear structures—principles long known to every designer. However, new perspectives are supplied by the eighth and tenth laws: Trust—namely, "In simplicity we trust"—and The One —"Simplicity is about subtracting the obvious and adding the meaningful". Yet, while the "obvious" qualities of a vegetable peeler—the grip, the blade, and the spacer—are simultaneously also "meaningful", it is scarcely feasible to display all the functions of digital products on their user interface. The fact is that digital technology is nearly

arbeiter eines Osloer Patentbüros, 1899 das kaiserlich-deutsche Büroklammer-Patent erhalten hatte, diente sie der norwegischen Bevölkerung 40 Jahre später im Zweiten Weltkrieg, angesteckt am Jackenkragen, als Symbol für den Widerstand gegen die deutsche Besatzung – heute ziert Oslo ein Denkmal mit einer überdimensionalen Büroklammer.

Das allen Modeströmungen widerstehende T-Shirt, ursprünglich Teil der Unterbekleidung, konnte sich, aufgrund der unübertroffenen Funktionalität seines „Nicht-Schnitts" und von James Dean und Marlon Brando exponiert, als modisches Statement etablieren: Indem es die Jugendidole in Kinohits der 1950er Jahre als Oberbekleidung trugen, verliehen sie dem Kleidungsstück die Aura von Rebellentum und Männlichkeit.

Aufgrund ihrer einfachen Formgebung und der universalen Einsetzbarkeit lassen sich Alltagsobjekte ihrem Kontext entwenden und funktional oder symbolisch neu aufladen. Wie anpassungsfähig an unseren Alltag sind hingegen digitale Medien? Lassen sich Interfaces zweckentfremden, sind ungeplante Weiterentwicklungen möglich? Das muss sich noch zeigen – bisher ist eher das Gegenteil der Fall. Die Produkte befriedigen nicht nur Bedürfnisse, sondern versuchen den Benutzer zu steuern, um den Warenstrom in Fluss zu halten: Kunden des Internet-Warenhauses Amazon erhalten Kaufempfehlungen, die zu ihrem Interessensprofil passen könnten, basierend auf bereits getätigten Einkäufen und früheren Suchbegriffen. Per User- und Eyetracking können

digitale Kommunikations- und Interaktionsgewohnheiten bis ins Detail analysiert werden, um gezielt neue Kaufangebote zu machen. Nichts wird Fortuna überlassen. Zufall wird höchstens absichtlich als *random effect* eingesetzt, etwa beim iPod Shuffle, dem Musikabspielgerät ohne Display, das die geladene Musik per Zufallsprinzip abspielt. Das bedeutet eine regelrechte Entmündigung des Konsumenten: Digitale Medien lassen Interaktion nur in vorgegebenem Rahmen zu, sie bieten dem User wenig Handlungsspielraum, um wirklich Neues zu entdecken oder eigenmächtig zu entwickeln. Um Neues zu generieren und Innovation zu schaffen, ist physisches Experimentieren jedoch unabdingbar. Selbst der Computerchip hätte ohne die Versuche mit den spezifischen materiellen Eigenschaften von Silizium nicht entstehen können.

Entgegen allen kulturpessimistischen Prophezeiungen wird das Verschwinden der Dinge in der digitalen Gesellschaft wohl noch eine Weile auf sich warten lassen. Und die analogen Gegenstände bleiben, was ihre Einfachheit und die damit verbundenen Vorteile anbelangt, vorerst unerreicht.

----

impossible to grasp, thus leaving us with no other choice but to rely on its simple interfaces.

Conversely, on account of their through-and-through simplicity, analogue objects of daily use have a fundamental advantage over their digital counterparts, namely the potential they bear on both the functional and semantic levels. This is exemplified in the ordinary plastic water bottles utilized around the globe. With the SODIS method of solar water disinfection, the common polyethylene terephthalate (PET) water bottle takes on a new function with far-reaching consequences in that it can be employed in third world countries to disinfect drinking water. For when PET bottles are filled with water and exposed to the sun for at least six hours, diarrhoea-causing germs are reliably killed off.

By contrast, the paper clip underwent an existential transformation not on the functional level but in terms of

semantics. Forty years after the Norwegian scientist and Oslo patent office employee Johan Vaaler obtained the German Imperial patent for the paper clip in 1899, it served as a symbol of Norway's resistance to German occupation in the Second World War when worn by Norwegian citizens on the lapel of their jackets. Today, this symbolic act of defiance is commemorated by a monument of an oversized paper clip located on the outskirts of Oslo.

Another example is the everenduring T-shirt. Originally considered an undergarment, it established itself as a fashion statement thanks to the unparalleled functionality of its boxy unconstructed cut and the exposure given to it by such cult figures as James Dean and Marlon Brando. Worn as outerwear in the hit films of the 1950s, these youth idols lent this item of clothing an aura of rebellion and masculinity that has remained intact to this very day.

One can see, then, that due to their simple form and universal applicability, everyday objects can be diverted from their original context and charged with new functionality or symbolism. But how adaptable to our daily life are digital media? Can interfaces be redirected for other purposes? Are unplanned transformations possible? That remains to be seen, for until now it has been more to the opposite. Rather than just catering to their needs, today's products seek to guide users to further purchases in order to maintain the flow of goods. Customers of the online store Amazon, for example, receive purchase recommendations corresponding to their personalized profile based on past buys and previously viewed items. By means of user and eye tracking, habits of digital communication and interaction can be analyzed in precise detail, mostly with the aim of producing targeted new sales offers. Nothing is left to chance, except

1 Marshall McLuhan: *Understanding Media: The Extensions of Man*. New York 1964.

2 John Maeda: *The Laws of Simplicity*, Cambridge, Mass., 2006.

----

1 Marshall McLuhan, *Understanding Media: The Extensions of Man* (New York: McGraw Hill, 1964).

2 John Maeda, *The Laws of Simplicity* (Cambridge, MA: MIT Press, 2006).

perhaps as an intentional effect as with the iPod Shuffle—the personal display-less music player that plays downloaded music in random order. As a result, consumers end up disenfranchised. Digital media only allow interaction within a given framework, offering users limited freedom to discover or develop something truly inventive on their own. Yet to generate something new and create innovation, physical experimentation remains indispensable. Even the computer chip could not have been produced without first testing the specific material properties of silicon.

Thus, despite the many culturally pessimistic prophecies alluding to the contrary, the disappearance of material things in digital society will likely be a long time coming. For as far as simplicity and its inherent advantages are concerned, analogue objects of the everyday remain unrivalled.

VERDICHTUNG /
COMPACTION

80

81

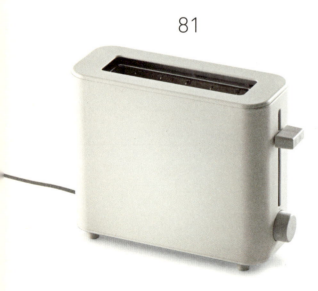

82

84

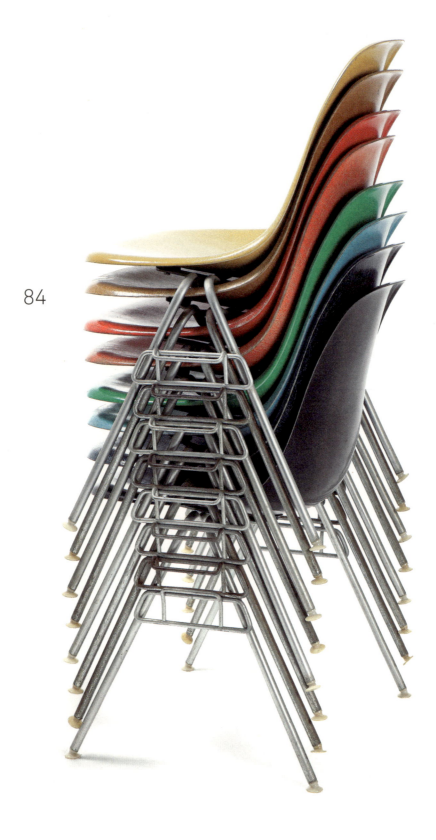

85

86

87

88

89

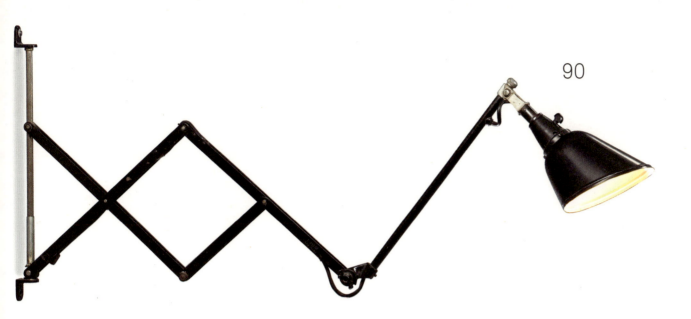

90

91

LEICHTIGKEIT /
LIGHTNESS

92

93

94

95

96

VERDICHTUNG / COMPACTION

80
Jonathan Paul Ive
Laptop
MacBook Air
2008
Apple Computer Inc., Cupertino, CA
1,9 x 32,5 x 22,7 cm
verschiedene Materialien / mixed media
Collection Vitra Design Museum, Weil am Rhein

Das Empfangen, Speichern, Visualisieren, Verarbeiten
und Weiterleiten unterschiedlichster Text-, Bild- und
sonstiger Daten auf einem fast bis zur Entmaterialisierung
verdichteten Raum ist zur unverzichtbaren Selbst-
verständlichkeit des Alltags geworden. Mit seinen nur
19,4 mm Höhe und 1,36 kg Gewicht setzte dieser Laptop
jedoch neue Maßstäbe.

The receipt, storage, visualization, processing, and trans-
mission of all manner of text, image, and other data in a
compact space verging on dematerialization has become
an indispensable and implicit part of daily life. Yet with
a thickness of just 19.4 millimetres and weight of 1.36
kilograms, this laptop managed to set new standards.

81
Naoto Fukasawa
Toaster
2007
Plus minus zero Co., Ltd., Tokyo
16,8 x 21,5 x 8 cm
verschiedene Materialien / mixed media
Collection Vitra Design Museum, Weil am Rhein

Erst beim zweiten Hinsehen fragt man sich, warum ein
Toaster für eine statt für zwei Scheiben Brot nicht schon
viel früher entwickelt worden ist – nicht nur weil er viel
selbstverständlicher ist und weil er Energie spart.

At second glance, one has to wonder why a toaster for
one instead of two slices of bread was not developed
much earlier—not only because it is much more intuitive
but also because it saves energy.

82
Marco Zanuso & Richard Sapper
Kofferradio / portable radio
TS 522
1964
Brionvega, Milano
13 x 23 x 13 cm
verschiedene Materialien / mixed media
Collection Studio 2

83
Charles-Edouard Jeanneret (Le Corbusier)
Hocker für den Pavillon du Brésil, Cité Internationale
Universitaire, Paris / stool for the Pavillon du Brésil, Cité
Internationale Universitaire, Paris
1953–59
43 x 33 x 25 cm
Holz / wood
Collection Vitra Design Museum, Weil am Rhein

Le Corbusier setzte dieses vielseitige Möbel zumeist in
kleineren Interieurs ein, wo es seine Dienste gleicher-
maßen als Hocker, Trittstufe oder Beistelltisch in drei
unterschiedlichen Höhen leisten sollte.

Le Corbusier primarily employed this versatile piece of
furniture in smaller interiors, where it served multiple
functions as a stool, step, or side table of three different
heights.

84
Charles & Ray Eames
8 Stapelstühle / stackable chairs
DSS
1954
Herman Miller Furniture Company, Zeeland, MI
80,5 x 55,8 x 54 cm (jeder Stuhl / each chair)
Fiberglas; verzinkter Stahl; Gummi; Kunststoff /

fiberglass; zinc-plated steel; rubber; plastic
Collection Vitra Design Museum, Weil am Rhein

85
Peter Bucher
Tablettwagen / trolley
1050000 (Part No.) / *127* (Serial No.)
1997
Bucher Leichtbau AG, Fällanden
105,5 x 83,4 x 32,6 cm
Aluminium, teilweise pulverbeschichtet / aluminum,
partly powder-coated
Schenkung Swiss International Air Lines, Basel
Collection Vitra Design Museum, Weil am Rhein

Gerätschaften in Flugzeugen müssen äußerst leicht und
platzsparend sein. In einem Volumen von 124 l tragen
die Schubfächer dieses Servierwagens mit patentierter
Rollenarretierung 45,5 kg Zuladung und sind von vorn wie
hinten zugänglich. Das doppelwandige Aluminiumgehäuse
hat eine gewisse isolierende Wirkung.

Equipment on board airplanes needs to be extremely light
and compact. With a volume of 124 litres and equipped
with patented wheel locks, the drawers of this trolley offer
a 45.5-kilogram load capacity and can be accessed from
both front and back. The double-walled aluminium housing
provides insulation.

86
Kleinstwagen / minicar
Tata Nano
2008
Tata Motors Ltd., Mumbai
1600 x 3100 x 1500 cm
verschiedene Materialien / mixed media
Tata Motors Ltd.

Mit seinem angekündigten Preis von 100 000 indischen
Rupien (ca. 1530,– €) gilt dieser Kleinstwagen des größten
indischen Autobauers als das billigste Serienauto der
Welt. Möglich wurde der Rekord durch ein Minimum an
Material- und Verarbeitungsaufwand. Während der *Nano*
bei der Sicherheit auch die europäischen Normen erfüllt,
ist hinsichtlich des Komforts die Eigeninitiative der Nutzer
gefordert. In der Benzinversion soll der Wagen 5 l auf 100
km verbrauchen; eine Hybridversion wird derzeit geplant.

With an advertised price of 100,000 Indian rupees
(approximately 1,530 euros), this microcar from India's
biggest auto manufacturer is considered the world's
cheapest mass-produced automobile. This record was
achieved by minimal expenditure on materials and
manufacturing. While the *Nano* also fulfils European
safety standards, it necessitates some initiative and
creativity on the part of the user as far as comfort is
concerned. The gasoline version of the car consumes
five litres for every 100 kilometres, with a hybrid version
currently planned for the future.

87
Enzo Mari
Stuhl / chair
Box
1976
Anonima Castelli spa, Ozzano dell'Emilia, BO
83 x 44,5 x 46,5 cm
Stahlrohr; Kunststoff / tubular steel; plastic
Collection Vitra Design Museum, Weil am Rhein

Der Stuhl wird in leuchtenden Farben als leichter Bau-
satz in einer Plastiktragetasche verkauft und lässt
sich mit wenigen Handgriffen zusammenstecken oder
auseinandernehmen.

Sold in brilliant hues as a simple self-assembly kit in a
plastic carrying case, this chair can be put together or
taken apart in just a few easy steps.

88
Wilhelm Wagenfeld
Behälter für Lebensmittel / food containers
Kubus
1938
Vereinigte Lausitzer Glaswerke, Weißwasser

22 x 27,5 x 18,5 cm
Pressglas / pressed glass
Collection Vitra Design Museum, Weil am Rhein

89
Philippe Starck
Tisch, Stuhl / table, chair
Mickville
1985
Driade spa, Fossadello di Caorso, PC
81 x 38 x 41,1 cm
Stahl; Epoxy / steel; epoxy
Collection Vitra Design Museum, Weil am Rhein

Das Möbel lässt sich flach zusammenlegen und dient als
Beistelltisch oder Stuhl, wobei der runde Tragegriff zur
drehbaren Lehne wird, die sich der Sitzrichtung anpasst.

This piece of furniture folds up flat and can serve as either
a side table or chair, with the round carrying handle
becoming a rotatable backrest that adjusts to the direction
of sitting.

90
Curt Fischer
ausziehbare Wandlampe / telescopic wall-light
No. 115 (*Midgard*)
1930
Industriewerk Auma, Ronneberger & Fischer, Auma i. Th. /
W. Goy & Co., Frankfurt/Main
50 x 47 x 16 cm
Eisen und Messing, schwarz emailliert und vernickelt /
iron and brass, black-enamelled and nickel-plated
Collection Vitra Design Museum, Weil am Rhein

91
anonym / anonymous
Feldbett aus dem Königshaus Hannover / camp bed of
the Royal House of Hannover
ca. 1800
70 x 87 x 211 cm
geschmiedetes Eisen; Ledermatratze / forged iron;
leather mattress
Collection Sebastian Jacobi

Mindestens so faszinierend wie die Gestalt dieses Feld-
betts, die Mies van der Rohes *Barcelona*-Möbel vorweg-
nimmt, ist sein einzigartiger Faltmechanismus. Das auf
40 cm Durchmesser und 1 m Länge komprimierte Gestell
gleicht auseinandergeklappt zunächst einem Schmetter-
ling mit hochgeschlagenen Flügeln. Erst nachdem diese
nochmals entfaltet sind, wird das Scherenkreuz sichtbar,
auf dessen obere Kanten Stäbe gesteckt und mit Schrauben fixiert werden, um die Konstruktion zu versteifen.

At least as fascinating as the design of this cot—which
anticipated Mies van der Rohe's *Barcelona* furniture—
is its unique folding mechanism. Folding up to a diameter
of 40 centimetres and length of 1 metre, the frame
initially resembles a butterfly with raised wings when
unfolded. Only after these are unfolded once again does
the scissor cross become visible, with rods screwed
into the top edges to reinforce the construction.

LEICHTIGKEIT / LIGHTNESS

92
Alfred Roth
Stapelstuhl / stackable chair
1933
Alfred Roth, Zürich
74,2 x 47,5 x 52,3 cm
Aluminium; aluminium
Collection Vitra Design Museum, Weil am Rhein

Der Entwurf entstand im Rahmen eines Wettbewerbs, den
die Alliance Aluminium Cie. für Aluminiummöbel ausge-
schrieben hatte, um neue Anwendungsmöglichkeiten des
Materials zu erschließen. Alfred Roth hatte sich mit drei
Modellen beteiligt, die beim Wettbewerb jedoch durch-
fielen, da die Verbindungen der Einzelteile über Nieten
und Schweißnähte den Belastungen nicht standhielten.

This design was created for a competition, sponsored

by Alliance Aluminium Cie. The competition was for aluminium furniture that opened up new areas of application for the material. Alfred Roth submitted three models, but all failed because the rivets and welds connecting the individual components did not hold up under the load test.

93

Alberto Meda
Stuhl / chair
LightLight
1986
Alias srl, Grumello del Monte, BG
70,5 x 53 x 47,5 cm
Kohlenstoffgewebe; Epoxidharz; Hartpolyurethanschaum / carbon fiber; epoxy resin; rigid polyurethane foam
Collection Vitra Design Museum, Weil am Rhein

Carbonfasern werden wegen ihrer Leichtigkeit und Bruchfestigkeit auch für Angelruten oder Tennisschläger verwendet. Um die Eigenschaften des Werkstoffs in den Vordergrund zu stellen, entwickelte Alberto Meda diesen im Volumen wie im Gewicht auf ein Minimum reduzierten Armlehnstuhl, der jedoch nie in Serie ging. Im Bereich von Sitz und Rückenlehne befindet sich im Innern der sich gegenläufig versteifenden Lagen aus Carbongewebe eine Wabenstruktur aus Hartpolyurethanschaum.

Lightweight and highly break-resistant, carbon fibre is also utilized in fishing rods and tennis rackets. Seeking to bring its material properties to the fore, Alberto Meda reduced both volume and weight to a minimum in the design of this armchair, though it never went into production. In the region of the seat and backrest, sheets of carbon fibre fabric are laid around a honeycomb core of rigid polyurethane foam.

94

Shigeru Ban
Stuhl / chair
Carbon Fiber Chair
2009
820 x 48,4 x 43,6 cm
Aluminium, Kohlefaser TENAX® (Teijin Ltd.) / aluminium; carbon fiber TENAX® (Teijin Ltd.)
Collection Alexander von Vegesack, Lessac-Confolens

Dieser Stuhl, der für die von Kenya Hara geleitete Ausstellung „Tokyo Fiber '09 – Senseware" entwickelt wurde, bietet eine hohe Stabilität bei einer größtmöglichen Leichtigkeit von nur 1800 g. Shigeru Ban nutzte dazu eine Symbiose zweier Materialien, die es erlaubt, jedes quantitativ zu minimieren. Während das Aluminium für einen flachen Rahmen im Kern den Druckkräften standhält, widerstehen den Zugkräften die zwei jeweils 0,25 mm dünnen, äußeren Carbonfaserschichten.

Developed for the "Tokyo Fiber '09 – Senseware" exhibition led by Kenya Hara, this chair combines a high level of stability with utmost lightness—just 1,800 grams. Shigeru Ban used a symbiosis of two materials that makes it possible to minimize the quantity of each. While the aluminium used for the inner flat frame resists the compressive pressure, the two outer carbon fibre layers—each just 0.25 millimetre thick—serve to resist the tractive forces.

95

Marcel Wanders
Sessel (Prototyp) / lounge chair (prototype)
Knotted Chair
1996
Wanders Wanders, Amsterdam
70 x 52 x 63 cm
Schnur; Kohlenstoffgewebe; Epoxidharz / cord; carbon fiber; epoxy resin
Collection Vitra Design Museum, Weil am Rhein

96

Giovanni Ponti
Stuhl / chair
No. 699 (Superleggera)
1951–57
Figli di Amedeo Cassina, Meda, MB
82,7 x 41 x 44,7 cm
lackierte Esche; Spanisches Rohr / lacquered ash;

India cane
Collection Vitra Design Museum, Weil am Rhein

Bei diesem Stuhl, den Gio Ponti selbst als „normalen", „wahren" Stuhl, als „Stuhl ohne Adjektive" beschrieb, verband der Designer seine eigene Forderung nach Beschränkung auf das absolut Notwendige mit seinem Interesse für klassische Formen. Er ließ sich von den schlichten, stabilen und leichten Stühlen inspirieren, wie sie eine ligurische Manufaktur mit großem Erfolg im 19. Jahrhundert herstellte.

In this chair—described by Gio Ponti himself as a "normal", "real" chair, as a "chair without adjectives"—the designer combined his own call for reduction to bare essentials with his interest in classical forms. He took inspiration from the simple, stable, and lightweight chairs produced with great success by nineteenth-century Ligurian artisans.

Dirk Baecker

WEGLASSEN ALS PARADOXE INTERVENTION /
OMISSION AS A PARADOXICAL INTERVENTION

Zwei Prinzipien beherrschen Natur und Gesellschaft, der selektive Umgang mit Energie und der selektive Umgang mit Sinn. Das eine nennen wir Arbeit, das andere Information. Arbeit, so sagen die Physiker, besteht darin, Energie aufzuwenden, um die Energie bestimmter Weltzustände auf die Energie anderer Weltzustände zu übertragen. Da Energie aufgewandt werden muss, um Energie zu gewinnen, gelingt es in der Regel, allenfalls einen Bruchteil der verfügbaren Energie aufzufangen und umzusetzen. Und da dies gleich zweimal gilt, einmal bei der Nutzung der Energie des Ausgangszustandes und ein zweites Mal bei der Übertragung dieser Energie auf den Zielzustand, ganz zu schweigen von der immer nur begrenzten Verfügung über den Träger der Arbeit, kann man sich leicht vorstellen, in welchen Energieüberschüssen wir uns bewegen müssen, wenn wir auch nur einen Bruchteil dieser Energie abzweigen und zu eigenen Zwecken verwenden wollen.

Vor diesem Hintergrund kann man sich mit der Biochemie nicht genug darüber wundern, dass es irgendwann vor vier Milliarden Jahren einzelligen Lebewesen gelungen ist, „einen kleinen Teil der Lichtenergie einzufangen und davon zu leben"[1]. Da dieser Vorgang für das Leben so fundamental und sein Gelingen zugleich evolutionär so unwahrscheinlich ist, hat man unwillkürlich den Eindruck, dass der Aufwand größer als der Ertrag sein muss, doch das kann physikalisch nicht stimmen. Also muss bereits hier das Prinzip der Reduktion wirksam geworden sein. Leben wurde möglich, weil es gelang, wegzulassen, was den Aufwand seiner Erzeugung und Fortsetzung hätte untragbar werden lassen. Anzapfen, ohne überwältigt zu werden, mitschwimmen, ohne mitgerissen zu werden, mitmachen, ohne sich unterwerfen zu müssen, das ist das Kunststück, das sich Leben nennt. Dann jedoch haben wir es bereits hier mit einem doppelten Reduktionismus zu tun. Es wird unterlassen, was die eigenen Ressourcen überfordert oder was Gegner und Widerstände auf den Plan ruft, mit denen man nicht fertig würde. Aber woher weiß der radikale Opportunismus, der sich hiermit dokumentiert, auf welche Gelegenheiten er sich konzentrieren muss?

Biologen sprechen von Nischen, in denen sich Parasiten einnisten, die das Milieu ausbeuten, so lange es geht. Diese Parasiten sind die Virtuosen des Weglassens. Sie rechnen damit, dass anderen die Energie fehlt, sich vor ihnen zu schützen. Sie entwickeln Techniken, die anderen davon zu überzeugen, dass sie selbst der Schutz sind, nach dem gesucht worden ist. Und sie rechnen mit einem grundsätzlichen Einverständnis, da es nichts gibt, was nicht in diesem Sinne parasitär wäre. Alles lebt extrem reduziert inmitten eines Überschusses, der sowohl schon da ist als auch sich immer wieder herstellt.

„Am Anfang ist das Rauschen", formuliert Michel Serres in seiner Philosophie des Parasiten, die einer der konsequentesten Versuche ist, die Prinzipien von Natur und Gesellschaft zusammenzudenken.[2] Nichts ist falscher als die Unterstellung einer *creatio ex nihilo*. Sie hilft zwar dabei, so zu tun, als habe man für einen

Two principles govern nature and society: the selective handling of energy and the selective handling of meaning. One is called work, the other information. According to the physicists, work involves expending energy in order to transfer the energy of certain states of the world to the energy of other states of the world. Thus, because a gain in energy necessitates the expenditure of energy, only a fraction of available energy tends to be captured and converted. And since this applies to two instances—once, in the use of the energy of the initial state, and, second, in the transfer of this energy to the target state, not to mention the ever-limited availability of the agent of the work involved—it is easy to imagine the energy surpluses needed to divert even just a fraction of energy and use it for our own purposes.

Against this background, one never ceases to be amazed—from a biochemical perspective—by the fact that single-celled organisms managed some four billion years ago "to capture a small part of ... light energy and live from it".[1] As this process is so fundamental to life yet so unlikely from an evolutionary standpoint, it instinctively seems that the expenditure would have to be greater than the yield, yet this is physically impossible. Hence, the principle of reduction must have already been in operation at the time. Life became viable because it was possible to omit whatever would have made the effort of its creation and reproduction prohibitive. Tapping into potential without being overwhelmed, going with the flow without getting carried away, joining in without being forced into submission—this is the trick called life. But then again, we are already dealing with a twofold reductionism here. Omissions are made to exclude exactly that which would overtax internal resources or unnecessarily stir up opponents and opposition and thus overwhelm defence capacities. But how does this radical opportunism know which opportunities to concentrate on?

Biologists speak of niches in which parasites lodge themselves and exploit the host environment as long as possible. These parasites are the virtuosos of omission. They reckon that others lack the energy to seek protection from them. Moreover, they develop techniques by which they convince others that they themselves are the very protection being sought. They count on a fundamental mutual agreement because there is nothing that would not be parasitic in this respect. Everything lives in extremely reduced fashion amidst a surplus that is already present at the start but also continuously regenerates itself.

"In the beginning was the noise", writes Michel Serres in his philosophy of the parasite, which constitutes one of the most systematic attempts to link the

Beginn jeden beliebigen Spielraum und könne seine Selektionen nach Belieben setzen, verstellt aber den Blick darauf, dass man sich tatsächlich in einer immer schon vielfach determinierten Welt bewegt. Herbert A. Simon sprach in diesem Zusammenhang von einer „empty world hypothesis", die es Managern und Designern erlaube, sich für ihre Projekte und Entwürfe den nötigen Raum zu verschaffen.[3] Unser Verständnis für dieses Abstraktionsmanöver darf uns jedoch nicht den Blick darauf verstellen, dass es nicht in einer leeren, sondern in einer vollen Welt stattfindet.

Denn was für die Energie gilt, die nur mithilfe von Arbeit in Arbeit verwandelt werden kann, gilt auch für den Sinn, mit dem die Gesellschaft es zu tun hat. Auch hier muss man Sinn investieren, um Sinn zu gewinnen, so als sei auch hier eine Ökonomie im Spiel, die nur dort einen Gewinn zulässt, wo ein Preis gezahlt wird. Die Idee des Mathematikers Claude E. Shannon bestand vor mehr als einem halben Jahrhundert darin, von einer Information nur dann zu reden, wenn eine Nachricht aus einem Möglichkeitenraum anderer Nachrichten ausgewählt wurde.[4] Denn ohne die Beobachtung dieser Selektivität hätte man es nicht mit einer Nachricht, sondern mit einem gleichsam stummen Weltzustand zu tun. Erst die Selektivität, erst der Umstand, dass die eine Nachricht unter so vielen anderen, ebenfalls möglichen Nachrichten ausgewählt wird, begründet die Lebendigkeit der Information. Denn nur so kann man zurückfragen, wer oder was für die Auswahl verantwortlich ist und welche der ausgeschlossenen

Möglichkeiten bei nächster Gelegenheit mindestens ebenso interessant wären.

Auch hier gilt der Satz, dass Sinn nur dort möglich ist, wo noch mehr Sinn vorhanden ist und im Moment nicht mitgeteilt wird. Die Auswahl macht den Sinn, ohne dass deswegen alles andere sinnlos würde. Alles andere ist ebenso sinnvoll wie die Auswahl, denn letztlich ist es gleichgültig, ob ich die Selektion auf das Eingeschlossene oder auf das Ausgeschlossene hin beobachte. Diese Gleichgültigkeit ist es, die mit der Entscheidung für eine Selektion überwunden werden muss. Und diese Entscheidung ist es, die dort Sinn macht, wo zuvor schon anderer Sinn war.

Der Gewinn von Energie aus Energie und von Sinn aus Sinn liefert uns zwei grandiose Tautologien und damit, wie der Anthropologe und Kybernetiker Gregory Bateson zu sagen pflegte, zwei robuste Erklärungsprinzipien, die im Zusammenhang unserer Suche nach einer Ethik und einem Design des Weglassens mindestens drei Einsichten enthalten.[5]

Erstens können wir aus ihnen ableiten, dass die Pointe der Arbeit wie der Information in der Selektion liegt und damit in einem Risiko, das derjenige, der die Selektion vornimmt, entweder trägt oder leugnet. Es könnte also sein, dass die Arbeit zwar ihren Teil erledigt, dafür jedoch an anderer Stelle noch mehr Arbeit macht. Und es könnte sein, dass eine Information nicht etwa bloß darüber aufklärt, was in der Welt der Fall ist, sondern einen Streit darüber auslöst, ob dies der Fall ist und was noch der Fall sein könnte.

----

principles of nature with those of society.[2] Nothing could be further from the truth than the assumption of a *creatio ex nihilo*. While this notion creates the helpful impression that one has enough leeway to choose his beginnings and define his selections freely, it clouds the reality that we operate in a world that has always been highly determined. Sure enough, Herbert A. Simon spoke in this regard of an "empty world hypothesis"[3] by which managers and designers create the space necessary to work on their projects and schemes. Our understanding of this manoeuvre of abstraction should not, however, make us lose sight of the fact that it occurs not in an empty but rather in a full world.

For the principle that energy can only be transformed into work through the application of work also applies to meaning in a societal context. Here too, meaning must be invested in order to gain meaning, since it is likewise governed by an economy that only allows gains where a price has been paid. Over half a century ago, the mathematician Claude E. Shannon posited the idea that information results when a message is selected from a set of other possible messages.[4] Without this selectivity, one would not be dealing with a message but with an essentially mute state of the world. Thus, it is selectivity—the fact that one message is chosen from so many other equally possible messages—that gives information its vitality. Only in this way can one check who or what is responsible for the selection and which of the excluded possibilities would be at least as interesting when the next opportunity presents itself.

Here as well, the statement holds that meaning is only possible where there is a surplus of meaning that is not currently being communicated. The selection creates the meaning without rendering everything else meaningless. Everything else is just as meaningful as the selection, for it ultimately does not matter whether one observes the selection in terms of what was included or what was excluded. This is the indifference that must be overcome in the decision to make a selection. And it is this decision that generates meaning where meaning already existed.

The gain of energy from energy and of meaning from meaning provides us with two grandiose tautologies and hence, as anthropologist and cybernetician Gregory Bateson used to say, two robust explanatory principles that contain at least three insights related to our search for an ethic and design of omission.[5]

First, we can deduce from them that the crux of both work and information lies in selection and thus bears a risk—a risk that is either embraced or disavowed by the one making the selec-

Zweitens sollte uns die strukturelle Ähnlichkeit zwischen dem selektiven Umgang mit Energie und dem selektiven Umgang mit Sinn nicht dazu verleiten, Energie und Sinn für dasselbe zu halten. Die Aussage der beiden Tautologien liegt vielmehr darin, Energie zwar in Energie und Sinn in Sinn, aber nicht Energie in Sinn und Sinn in Energie verwandeln zu können. Was wir für sinnvoll halten, ist damit noch nicht getan. Und was getan ist, muss deshalb noch nicht sinnvoll sein. Diesen Unterschied, der mindestens so elementar ist wie Energie und Sinn, behalten wir uns vor, und sei es nur, um präzise darauf achten zu können, wann welche Information in Arbeit umgesetzt wird und wann welche Arbeit zu einer Information führt. Keine Frage, jeder Parasit ist ein Beobachter und jeder Beobachter ein Parasit. Und dennoch halten wir daran fest, dass diese beiden Rollen auch immer wieder auseinanderfallen. Wir leben in und mit einer Gesellschaft der Parasiten und Beobachter, die dort den Überschuss garantieren, wo sie selber ihre Selektionen setzen.

Die Maxime des Weglassens hat daher drittens die Form einer paradoxen Intervention. Sie fordert das Unvermeidliche. Ohne ein Weglassen gelingt weder eine Arbeit noch eine Information. Wenn jedoch zum Weglassen aufgefordert wird, springt der Blick der Beobachter, unmittelbar verfolgt von Parasiten, auf das Weggelassene. In diesem Moment wird es für Ethiker wie für Designer interessant. Der Ethiker interessiert sich für den weggelassenen Sinn und fragt sich, ob und wann das Ausgeschlossene wieder eingeschlossen werden sollte. Und der Designer überprüft die weggelassene Energie und stellt die Frage nach einem eventuellen Korrekturbedarf der damit einhergehenden Ökonomie.

Beide jedoch sind sich in der Einschätzung der Maxime einig. *Less is more*, wenn man das Gleichheitszeichen in all seiner Paradoxie wörtlich nimmt. Denn die Kunst wie die Moral liegen hier nicht etwa in der kleinen und vermeintlich armen oder schwachen Lösung, sondern im Überschuss an Energie und Sinn, den diese Lösung offenbart. Die Kunst liegt in der Reduktion, die die Welt mit vorführt. Dann ist die arme und schwache eine reiche und starke Lösung. Und dann kippt die Ökonomie der Lösung zurück in die Ökologie einer Problemstellung, die sich so und anders bearbeiten lässt.

1 Gottfried Schatz: „Der lebenspendende Strom. Wie Lebewesen sich die Energie des Sonnenlichts teilen", in: *Neue Zürcher Zeitung*, 2. November 2009.

2 Michel Serres: *Der Parasit*, übers. v. Michael Bischof, Frankfurt a.M. 1981, S. 28.

3 Herbert A. Simon: *The Sciences of the Artificial*, 2. Aufl., Cambridge, Mass. 1981, S. 221.

4 Claude E. Shannon: „A Mathematical Theory of Communication", in: *Bell System Technical Journal*, Nr. 27, 1948, 379–423, 623–656.

5 Gregory Bateson: *Mind and Nature. A Necessary Unity*, New York 1979.

----

1 Gottfried Schatz, "Der lebenspendende Strom: Wie Lebewesen sich die Energie des Sonnenlichts teilen", *Neue Zürcher Zeitung*, 2 November 2009.

2 Michel Serres, *Le parasite* (Paris: Grasset, 1980), 23.

3 Herbert A. Simon, *The Sciences of the Artificial*, 2nd ed. (Cambridge, MA: MIT Press, 1981), 221.

4 Claude E. Shannon, "A Mathematical Theory of Communication", *Bell System Technical Journal* 27 (1948), 379–423, 623–656.

5 Gregory Bateson, *Mind and Nature: A Necessary Unity* (New York: Dutton, 1979).

----

tion. Hence, it could be that the work does its part but ends up making even more work elsewhere in the process. And it could be that a piece of information does not merely explain what the case is in the world but prompts a dispute over whether this is the case and what else might be the case.

Second, the structural similarity between the selective handling of energy and the selective handling of meaning should not mislead us into regarding energy and meaning as the same thing. Rather, the essence of the two tautologies lies in being able to transform energy into energy and meaning into meaning, but not energy into meaning and meaning into energy. What we consider meaningful is thus yet to be done. And what has been done is nonetheless yet to be meaningful. We assert our right to this difference—a difference that is at least as fundamental as energy and meaning, even if it merely enables us to pay precise attention to when certain information is converted into work and when certain work leads to information. There is no question about it: each parasite is an observer and each observer is a parasite. Yet, nevertheless, we remain firmly convinced that these two roles continually part ways. We live in and with a society of parasites and observers that guarantee the surplus where they themselves define their selections.

Hence, thirdly, the maxim of omission takes the form of a paradoxical intervention. It demands the inevitable. Without omission, neither work nor information is possible. Yet when omission is called for, the attention of observers abruptly shifts to what was omitted, closely followed by parasites. Such moments prove interesting for ethicists as well as for designers. The ethicist is interested in the omitted meaning and asks if and when the excluded might be included again, while the designer examines the omitted energy and enquires about a potential need to correct the resulting economy.

Nevertheless, both agree in their assessment of the maxim. Less is more when one takes the equal sign literally in the full breadth of its paradoxical nature. For neither the art nor the moral lies in the small and supposedly poor or weak solution but in the surplus of energy and meaning that this solution reveals. The art lies in the reduction demonstrated by the world. Then the poor and weak solution is a rich and strong one. And then the economy of the solution shifts back into the ecology of a problem that can thus, and otherwise, be addressed.

GEOMETRIE /
GEOMETRY

97

98

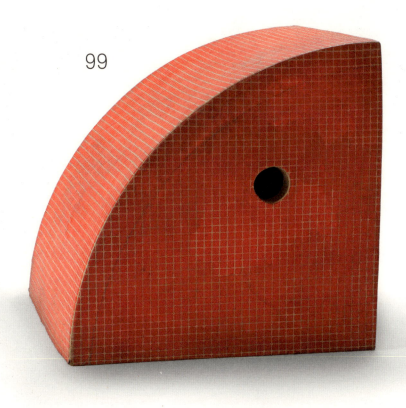

99

101

102

103

104

105

106

107

ABSTRAKTION /
ABSTRACTION

108

109

110

111

112

113

114

115

116

117

118

119

AUFLÖSUNG /
DISSOLUTION

120

121

122

123

124

125

126

127

128

TRANSPARENZ /
TRANSPARENCY

129

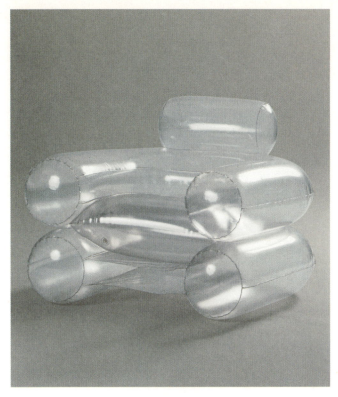

130

131

132

133

134

ZEICHEN /
SIGN

レンズには絶対に触れないでください。
NEVER TOUCH THE LENS.
NE JAMAIS TOUCHER LA LENTILLE.
請不要觸摸雷射讀解頭。
NON TOCCARE LA LENTE.

135

136

137

138

139

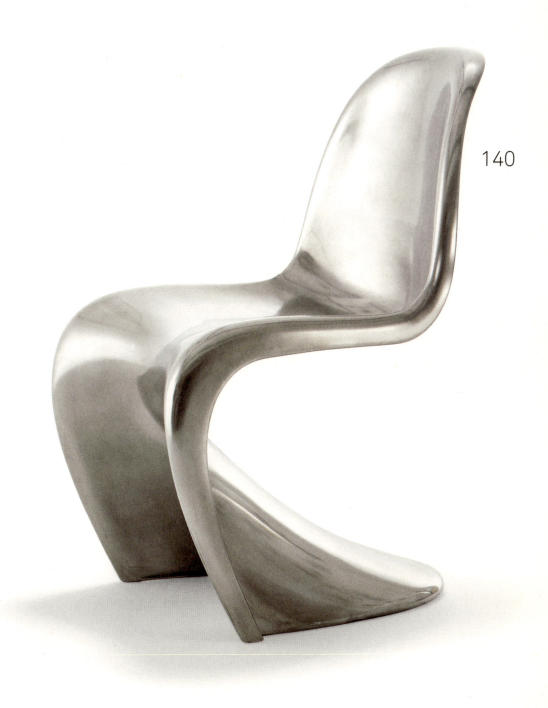

140

141

142

143

144

145

146

147

97

Maarten Van Severen
Bücherregal / bookshelf
2 Meter Boeken
1993
Maarten Van Severen, Gent
33,5 x 253,2 x 24,2 cm
Aluminium; aluminium
Collection Vitra Design Museum, Weil am Rhein

98

Gymnastikball / gym ball
undatiert / undated
aktivshop, Rheine
65 x 65 x 65 cm
Polyvinylchlorid / Polyvinyl chloride (PVC)
Collection Mathias Schwartz-Clauss

„Der Kopf ist rund, damit das Denken die Richtung ändern kann", bemerkte der französische Künstler Francis Picabia. Und so ist es auch mit dem Sitzen: Gesundes Sitzen erfordert möglichst viel Bewegung, ein steifer Sitz entspricht nicht der menschlichen Anatomie. Doch aus medizinischer Sicht sollte auch die Positionsveränderung auf einem Gymnastikball zeitlich beschränkt sein, zumal die Instabilität erhebliche Unfallgefahr birgt.

"The head is round so that thinking can change direction", remarked the French artist Francis Picabia. And so it is with sitting as well. Rigid seats are incompatible with the human anatomy, while healthy sitting requires freedom of movement. Yet from a medical perspective, so-called active sitting on an exercise ball should only be practised for limited periods of time due to the risk of injury.

99

G. Ceretti, P. Derossi, R. Rosso (Gruppo Strum)
Sessel / easy chair
Tornerai
1969
Gufram srl, Balangero, TO
84 x 85 x 88 cm
Guflex-Polyurethanschaum; Guflac-Lack /
Guflex polyurethane foam; Guflac lacquer
Collection Vitra Design Museum, Weil am Rhein

Wenn Körpergewicht und Gesäßumfang sich dem Koordinatensystem dieses geometrischen Volumens einschreiben, verformt es sich zum bequemen Armsessel.

When body weight and hip circumference inscribe themselves into the geometric volume's internal coordinate system, it compresses into a comfortable armchair.

100

Peter Hamburger & Ingo Maurer
Bodenlampe / floor lamp
Light Structure
1970
Design M, München
47 x 57 x 52,5 cm
Elektrodraht; Glas; Kunststoff / electric wire; glass; plastic
Collection Vitra Design Museum, Weil am Rhein

101

Erich Dieckmann
Kinderarmlehnstuhl / children's armchair
1928
Staatliche Bauhochschule Weimar
54,5 x 36,5 x 35 cm
lackiertes Buchenholz; lackiertes Sperrholz / lacqueres beechwood; lacquered plywood
Collection Alexander von Vegesack, Lessac-Confolens

Ausgehend von klaren, geometrischen Modulen, wie er sie am Weimarer Bauhaus kennen gelernt hatte, entwickelte Erich Dieckmann in den 1920er Jahren schlichte, solide Möbel für die handwerkliche Serienproduktion.

Based on the clear geometric modules he had become acquainted with at the Weimar Bauhaus, Erich Dieckmann created throughout the 1920s simple, solid furniture for serial manufacture by hand.

102

Gerrit T. Rietveld
Armsessel / armchair
Roodblauwe stoel
1918
G. van de Groenekan, Utrecht
86 x 65,8 x 82 cm
lackiertes Holz / lacquered wood
Collection Vitra Design Museum, Weil am Rhein

Die Künstler des De Stijl um Theo van Doesburg und Piet Mondrian erhoben diese geometrische Abstraktion eines Sessels als Komposition aus Flächen und Linien zu ihrem Manifest und Vorbild für die „(abstrakt-realistischen) Bilder in unserem zukünftigen Interieur". Statt eines Prototyps schuf Gerrit Rietveld mehrere Varianten, in denen er die Abmessungen immer wieder neu justierte. Die erste farbige Fassung entstand um 1923.

The artists of the De Stijl movement, centred around Theo van Doesburg and Piet Mondrian, embraced Gerrit Rietveld's geometric abstraction of an armchair composed of planes and lines as their manifesto and model for the "(abstract-real) images of our future interior". Instead of a prototype, Rietveld created multiple variants, each time making slight adjustments to the dimensions. The first coloured version appeared around 1923.

103

Charles & Ray Eames / Eero Saarinen
Architekturmodell 1:15 / architectural model 1:15
Case Study House No. 8 (Eames House)
1945–49
(Modellbau durch / model construction by:
Vitra Design Museum, 1997)
43,7 x 76,7 x 189,7 cm
PVC; Polystyrol / PVC; polystyrene
Collection Vitra Design Museum, Weil am Rhein

Vier Jahre nach Ende des II. Weltkrieges setzte das *Eames-Haus* als Flaggschiff des „Case Study House Program" der kalifornischen Zeitschrift *Arts & Architecture* einen neuen, amerikanischen Maßstab in der Architektur: Konzipiert nach dem Prinzip eines modularen Baukastens für den Eigenbau, trägt diese betont rechtwinklige Konstruktion aus nackten, industriell gefertigten Stahlteilen die Wand- und Fensterelemente wie austauschbare Kulissen, in denen Bewohner und Möbel zu dreidimensionalen Motiven werden.

Four years after the Second World War, the *Eames House* set a new standard for American architecture as the flagship of the "Case Study House Program" of the Californian magazine *Arts & Architecture*. Conceived according to the principle of modular design for do-it-yourself construction, the rectangular grid of exposed, industrially fabricated steel components supports the wall and window units as if they were interchangeable scenery elements in which the occupants and furniture themselves become three-dimensional motifs.

104

Paolo Tilche
Tischlampe / table lamp
No. 3H
1971
Sirrah spa, Imola, BO
16 x 18,5 x 16 cm
verchromtes Metall; lackiertes Metall /
chrome-plated metal; lacquered metal
Collection Vitra Design Museum, Weil am Rhein

105

Ettore Sottsass jr.
Tischlampe / table lamp
Halo Click
ca. 1988
Philips, Eindhoven
44,5 x 13 x 39,2 cm
lackiertes Metall / lacquered metal
Collection Vitra Design Museum, Weil am Rhein

106

Verner Panton
Likörwagen / liquor cart
Barboy
1963
A. Sommer, Plüdershausen
76,5 x 38 x 38 cm
Schichtholz, verformt und lackiert; Metall; Kunststoff /
laminated wood moulded and lacquered; metal; plastic
Collection Vitra Design Museum, Weil am Rhein

107

Donald Judd
Stuhl / chair
No. 84/8
1997
Donald Judd Furniture ™, © Judd Foundation,
New York, NY / Marfa, TX
76,2 x 38,1 x 38,1 cm
Kiefernholz / pine wood
Collection Alexander von Vegesack, Lessac-Confolens

Mit seinen einfachen geometrischen Körpern als offene oder geschlossene Volumen im Raum gilt der Künstler Donald Judd als ein Hauptvertreter des Minimalismus. Seine ersten Stühle entwarf er für ein Anwesen in Texas, das er 1977 als Wohn- und Arbeitsstätte bezog, ab 1982 wurden seine Möbel auch in kleinen Auflagen produziert. Doch Judd bestand strikt auf deren Trennung von seinem künstlerischen Werk: „Möbeln und Architektur kann man sich nur als solchen nähern; man kann ihnen Kunst nicht aufzwingen. Aber wenn man ihre Eigenart, ihren Charakter ernsthaft berücksichtigt, entsteht Kunst, ja fast so etwas wie Kunst an sich." * schrieb er 1985. (Bei dem hier abgebildeten Stuhl handelt es sich um den Prototypen der Serie, zu der das für den Leihgeber angefertigte Exponat, das nicht rechtzeitig fotografiert werden konnte, gehört.)

* Donald Judd: *Donald Judd Möbel Furniture*,
Zürich 1986, o.S.

With his simple geometric figures made of open or closed volumes in space, artist Donald Judd is considered one of the leading representatives of Minimalism. He designed his first chairs for the estate in Texas in which he lived and worked from 1977. In 1982, his furniture designs began to be produced in small editions. Yet Judd insisted on their strict separation from his artistic work, as he wrote in 1985: "Furniture and architecture can only be approached as such. Art cannot be imposed upon them. If their nature is seriously considered, the art will occur, even art close to art itself." * (Depicted here is the prototype of the series to which the work on loan to the exhibition belongs. The latter could not be photographed in time for publication.)

* Donald Judd, *Donald Judd Möbel Furniture* (Zurich: Arche Verlag AG, Raabe + Vitali, 1986), unpaginated.

ABSTRAKTION / ABSTRACTION

108

Luigi Colani
Sitzgerät / seating device
Colani
1972
Top System Burkhard Lübke, Gütersloh
65,5 x 55,7 x 65 cm
Polyethylen / polyethylene
Collection Vitra Design Museum, Weil am Rhein

Bei diesem biomorphen Möbel schmiegt sich der Körper in jeder Haltung an abgerundete Kanten und ansatzlose Übergänge. Der Sitz ist mit einem Pult kombiniert, das in umgekehrter Sitzrichtung als Rückenlehne dient.

With this biomorphic design, the body nestles against the rounded edges and seamless transitions in whichever chosen posture. The seat is combined with a desk that functions as a backrest in the reverse direction.

109

Friedrich (Frederick) J. Kiesler
Schaukelstuhl / rocking chair
(für / for Peggy Guggenheim's Art of This Century Gallery)
1942
73,9 x 40,5 x 84,7 cm
Esche; Linoleum / ash; linoleum
Collection Vitra Design Museum, Weil am Rhein

Für Peggy Guggenheims New Yorker Galerie Art of This
Century entwarf Friedrich Kiesler einen sphärisch ge-
krümmten Raum sowie verschiedene Varianten dieses
Möbels, das als bequemer Schaukelstuhl oder, auf die
Seite gelegt, als Podest für die Exponate diente.

For Peggy Guggenheim's Art of This Century Gallery in
New York, Friedrich Kiesler designed a spherically curved
interior as well as multiple variations of this piece of
furniture, which served as a comfortable rocking chair or,
placed on its side, as a base for exhibits.

110

Donald R. Knorr
Stuhl / chair
No. 132U
1948
Knoll Associates, Inc., New York, NY
71,7 x 55,7 x 53,3 cm
lackiertes Stahlblech; lackiertes Stahlrohr / lacquered
sheet steel; lacquered tubular steel
Collection Vitra Design Museum, Weil am Rhein

111

Arne Jacobsen
Stapelstuhl / stackable chair
No. 3100 (Ameise / The Ant)
1952
Fritz Hansens Eft. A/S, København
77 x 52 x 51,5 cm
geformtes Sperrholz; Stahl; Gummi / molded plywood;
steel; rubber
Collection Vitra Design Museum, Weil am Rhein

Dank zusätzlicher Furnierlagen ist die schöne, schlanke
Taille, die dem Stuhl den Namen *Ameise* einbrachte und
eine gewisse Flexibilität der Rückenlehne bewirkt, der
Beanspruchung des Materials an dieser empfindlichen
Stelle gewachsen. Die formale und funktionale Vereinheit-
lichung, die auch den Produktionsaufwand reduziert, geht
jedoch, verglichen etwa mit den Eames'schen Lösungen,
zulasten des Sitzkomforts.

Earning it the name *Ant* and effecting a certain flexibility in
the backrest, the elegant, slender waist of this chair was
reinforced with additional layers of veneer to accommodate
the stress on the materials at this particularly vulnerable
point. The formal and functional uniformity reduced
production costs but came at the expense of seating
comfort compared to other solutions, such as those
by the Eameses.

112

Sori Yanagi
Hocker / stool
Butterfly
1954
Tendo Mokko Co., Ltd., Tokyo
41,5 x 47,5 x 34,2 cm
gebogenes Sperrholz; Messing / molded plywood; brass
Collection Alexander von Vegesack, Lessac-Confolens

Das erhöhte Sitzen war der japanischen Kultur bis weit
ins 20. Jahrhundert noch sehr fremd. Wie zwei geöffnete
Hände, die etwas Wertvolles präsentieren, formuliert
dieser aus zwei identischen Bugholzteilen zusammen-
gesetzte Hocker eine Gestalt, die an das japanische
Schriftzeichen für „Himmel" erinnert.

Elevated sitting remained foreign to Japanese culture
until well into the twentieth century. Like two open hands
presenting something of value, this stool—composed
of two identical pieces of bent wood—produces a form
reminiscent of the Japanese character for "heaven".

113

Charles & Ray Eames
Dreibeiniger Stuhl, Experiment /
3-legged chair, experimental piece
1945
Molded Plywood Division, Evans Products Co., Venice, CA
76,5 x 51,6 x 55,3 cm
geformtes Sperrholz, gefärbt; lackierter Stahlrundstab;
Gummi; Metall / molded plywood, dyed; lacquered steel
rod; rubber; metal
Collection Vitra Design Museum, Weil am Rhein

An dieser experimentellen, dreibeinigen Variante des etwa
zeitgleich realisierten Stuhls *DCM* wird die kompromiss-
lose Konzentration auf die optimale Funktionstüchtigkeit
bei minimalem Materialaufwand besonders deutlich.

In this experimental three-legged variant of the *DCM* chair
that was realized around the same time, the Eameses' un-
compromising focus on optimal functionality paired with
minimal use of materials becomes especially apparent.

114

Alvar Aalto
Kinderstuhl / children's chair
No. 103
1931/32
Oy Huonekalu-ja Rakennustyötehdas Ab, Turku
58 x 34 x 49 cm
laminiertes Birkenholz, gebogen; gebogenes Sperrholz,
lackiert / bent laminated birch; bent plywood, lacquered
Collection Vitra Design Museum, Weil am Rhein

Wie die meisten Zeitgenossen empfand Alvar Aalto das
von der Bauhaus-Avantgarde gefeierte Stahlrohr als zu
kalt und unangenehm für den täglichen Gebrauch. Gleich-
wohl war er fasziniert von den dynamischen Konstrukti-
onsmöglichkeiten, die das Material eröffnete. Mit diesem
Stuhl aus Sperrholz, das den Belastungen besser standhält als gebogenes Massivholz, gelang ihm der erste
hölzerne Freischwinger. Bemerkenswert ist, dass der Entwurf eigens für Kinder entwickelt wurde und nicht einfach
einen Erwachsenen-Stuhl verkleinert.

Like most of his contemporaries, Alvar Aalto found the
tubular steel celebrated by the Bauhaus avant-garde to
be too cold and uncomfortable for everyday use. Nevertheless, he was fascinated by the dynamic construction
possibilities opened up by the material. Choosing plywood
over bent solid wood for its superior ability to withstand
stress, he succeeded in creating the first cantilevered
chair made of wood. It is worth noting that the version
depicted was developed specifically for children and not
simply as a miniaturized adult chair.

115

Isamu Noguchi
Couchtisch / coffee table
IN-52
1944
Herman Miller Furniture Co., Zeeland, MI
40 x 127,3 x 90,5 cm
gefärbtes Birkensperrholz; Stahl /
laminated birch, ebonized; steel
Collection Vitra Design Museum, Weil am Rhein

116

Serge Mouille
Wandlampe / wall lamp
Applique à deux bras pivotants
1954
Atelier Serge Mouille, Paris
160 x 198 x 29 cm
lackierter Stahl; Messing / lacquered steel; brass
Collection Alexander von Vegesack, Lessac-Confolens

117

Heinz & Bodo Rasch
Stuhl / chair
Sitzgeiststuhl
1927
(Nachbau durch / reproduction by: Vitra Design Museum,
2010)
88,8 x 43,6 x 47,2 cm

lackiertes Sperrholz / lacquered plywood
Collection Vitra Design Museum, Weil am Rhein

Ein Jahr nach dem Erscheinen des ersten hinterbeinlosen
Stuhls von Mart Stam fassten die Brüder Rasch mit
diesem Entwurf ihre Überlegungen zu Konstruktion, Anatomie und Ergonomie zusammen. Die ungewöhnliche,
Gerrit Rietvelds *Zig zag*-Stuhl vorwegnehmende Silhouette
der Seitenrahmen, die die leicht federnden Sitz- und
Rückenflächen halten, ist von der Gestalt eines Menschen
abgeleitet, der in der Kniebeuge verharrt. Wegen seines
Komforts wurde der Stuhl zwar für öffentliche Verkehrs-
mittel empfohlen, aber schließlich doch nur in geringer
Stückzahl produziert.

One year after the appearance of the first chair with no
back legs by Mart Stam, the Rasch Brothers summed up
their own deliberations on construction, anatomy, and
ergonomics with this design. Anticipating Gerrit Rietveld's
Zig zag chair, the unusual silhouette of the side frames
holding the slightly flexible seat and back is derived from
the figure of a person bending at the knee. Due to its comfort, the chair was even recommended for use in public
transportation, but in the end only a limited quantity was
produced.

118

Philippe Starck
Zahnbürste / tooth-brush
Fluocaril Starck
1990
Laboratoires pharmaceutiques Goupil SA, Rungis
30,4 x 9,4 x 6,5 cm
Kunststoff / plastic
Collection Vitra Design Museum, Weil am Rhein

Das stromlinienförmige Horn ist fast ein Markenzeichen
Philippe Starcks, so universell verwendet er diese griffige
Form in seiner Gestaltung. Hier überzeugt es jedoch
weniger in seiner Funktion denn als gestalterisches
Statement zur organischen Form. Denn obwohl der Schaft
gut in der Hand liegt, bietet er den heftigen Bewegungen
beim Bürsten keinen rechten Widerstand.

The streamlined horn has become something of a
trademark for Philippe Starck, considering how widely
he has applied this easy-to-grip shape in his designs.
In this case, however, it is less compelling in its function
than as an aesthetic statement on organic form. Although
the shaft fits comfortably in the hand, it offers no real
resistance to the vigorous motions of brushing.

AUFLÖSUNG / DISSOLUTION

119

Isamu Noguchi
Hängeleuchte / hanging lamp
Akari 120A
ca. 1955
Ozeki & Co., Ltd., Gifu
120 x 120 x 120 cm
Bambus; Papier; Metall / bamboo; paper; metal
Collection Vitra Design Museum, Weil am Rhein

120

Mario Asnago & Claudio Vender
Stuhl / chair
(Stuhl für die *Bar Moka*) / (chair for *Bar Moka*)
1939
90 x 32,7 x 37,5 cm
Stahlrohr, lackiert; Binsengeflecht /
tubular steel, lacquered; rush matting
Collection Sebastian Jacobi

Für eine beengte Mailänder Bar, die Mario Asnago und
Claudio Vender durch die Verspiegelung einer Wand
optisch erweiterten, entstand dieser Stuhl mit seiner
filigranen Gestalt und derart reduzierten Abmessungen,
dass gerade genug Bequemlichkeit für einen Espresso
und einen kleinen Schwatz übrig bleibt.

For a cramped Milanese bar, Mario Asnago and Claudio
Vender visually expanded the space with a mirrored wall
and created this filigree chair with reduced dimensions
that provided just enough comfort for an espresso and a
quick chat.

121
Charles & Ray Eames
Stuhl, Experiment / chair, experimental piece
Minimum Chair
1948
Eames Office, Venice, CA
85,5 x 42 x 44 cm
Stahlrundstab; gelochtes Metall, lackiert /
steel rod; perforated metal, lacquered
Collection Vitra Design Museum, Weil am Rhein

Für den Wettbewerb des Museum of Modern Art in New York „International Competition for Low-Cost Furniture Design" ließen Charles und Ray Eames ihre Erkenntnisse aus der Entwicklung von Sperrholzstühlen in eine Reihe experimenteller Möbel aus Metall einfließen. Den Vorgaben entsprechend schufen sie hier mit einem Minimum an Material einen preiswerten, platzsparenden, aber immer noch bequemen Sitz.

For the "International Competition for Low-Cost Furniture Design" sponsored by the Museum of Modern Art in New York, Charles and Ray Eames made use of the know-how they had gained from working with plywood chairs in order to create a series of experimental furniture pieces made out of metal. In accordance with the competition guidelines, they utilized a minimal amount of material to produce a low-cost, space-saving yet comfortable seat.

122
Shiro Kuramata
Armsessel / armchair
How High The Moon
1986
Vitra AG, Basel
72,5 x 95 x 83,2 cm
vernickeltes Streckmetall / nickeled wire mesh
Collection Vitra Design Museum, Weil am Rhein

„Die Gravitation ist eine Kraft, die über uns steht und alle Dinge auf Erden kontrolliert [...] einschließlich der Ideologien", aber „das Nichts regiert alles". * In diesem Widerspruch, der symptomatisch für den Dualismus in der shintoistischen Ethik und Ästhetik ist, formulierte Shiro Kuramata ein zentrales Motiv seiner Arbeit, für das er poetische Bilder aus Transparenz und Schwerkraft fand.

* *Shiro Kuramata: 1934–1991*, hrsg. v. Michiko Aikawa, Ausst.-Katalog, Hara Museum of Contemporary Art, Tokio 1996, S. 140, 153.

"Gravitation is a force that stands over us and keeps all things on this earth under its control ... including ideology", but "nothingness rules over everything". * With this contradiction capturing the dualism of the Shinto ethic and aesthetic, Shiro Kuramata formulates one of the central motifs of his oeuvre, which includes poetic images of transparency and gravity.

* *Shiro Kuramata: 1934–1991*, ed. Michiko Aikawa, exhibition catalogue (Tokyo: Hara Museum of Contemporary Art, 1996), 140, 153.

123
Tokujin Yoshioka
Stuhl / chair
Honey-Pop
2001
Tokujin Yoshioka Design, Tokyo
68,8 x 52,5 x 67,2 cm
Pergamentpapier / glassine paper
Collection Alexander von Vegesack, Lessac-Confolens

Kennzeichnend für Yoshiokas Entwürfe ist ihre konsequente Konzentration auf das Material, dem unerwartete Eigenschaften entlockt werden, um dem Objekt und dem Umgang mit ihm neue Bedeutung zu verleihen. Yoshiokas Lehrer waren Kuramata und Miyake, dessen Studio er beitrat, als dort mit gefaltetem Stoff experimentiert wurde.

Characteristic of Tokujin Yoshioka's designs is their systematic focus on the material, eliciting unanticipated properties that give new meaning to the object and our interactions with it. Yoshioka's mentors were Shiro Kuramata and Issey Miyake, whose studio he joined during its experimentations with folded fabric.

124
Marcel Breuer
Armsessel / armchair
B 3 (Wassily)
1925
Standard-Möbel Lengyel & Co., Berlin
72,5 x 76,5 x 69,5 cm
vernickeltes Stahlrohr; Stoff (Eisengarn) /
nickeled tubular steel; fabric (polished yarn)
Collection Alexander von Vegesack, Lessac-Confolens

Dieses erste Wohnmöbel aus Stahlrohr – ein Sessel, dessen Korpus zum Skelett abgemagert ist, und der sich noch in den (heute verlorenen) Reflexen der Verchromung und des Eisengarnbezugs aufzulösen scheint – erschien der Avantgarde wie ein Befreiungsschlag: endlich Luft, Dynamik, Klarheit, Leichtigkeit und die Vision einer preiswerten, soliden und neutralen Einrichtung für alle. In der öffentlichen Wahrnehmung wurde dieses Objekt wie kein anderes zum Symbol für das Bauhaus.

The very first piece of tubular steel furniture designed for the home, this armchair—whose physical presence is stripped down to a skeleton and seems to further dissipate in the (nowadays lost) reflections of the chrome plating and bands of steel-thread fabric—was embraced by the avant-garde as a burst of liberation: finally there was air, dynamics, clarity, lightness, and a vision of affordable, solid, and neutral furniture for all. In the public perception, this object came to symbolize the Bauhaus like no other.

125
Mart Stam
Stuhl (Reedition)
W1
1926
Tecta, Lauenförde
83,5 x 46 x 53 cm
lackiertes Stahlrohr; Baumwolle /
lacquered tubular steel; cotton
Collection Vitra Design Museum, Weil am Rhein

Nachdem der russische Künstler El Lissitzky mit seinem *Wolkenbügel* die kühne Idee eines in luftiger Höhe wie schwerelos auskragenden Gebäudes veröffentlicht hatte, nutzte der Architekt Mart Stam die Stabilität des Stahlrohrs für den ersten Stuhl, dessen Sitz nur von Vorderbeinen getragen wird. In seiner endlosen Schlaufe scheint die Figur dieses Objekts über den Boden zu gleiten.

Following Russian artist El Lissitzky's bold concept for buildings weightlessly projecting into the lofty heights (*Wolkenbügel*, "Cloud-Hangers"), architect Mart Stam made use of the stability of tubular steel for the first chair with a seat borne solely by its front legs. In its infinite loop, the figure of the chair seems to glide across the floor.

126
Ludwig Mies van der Rohe
Armlehnstuhl
MR 50 (Brno)
1929
Berliner Metallgewerbe, Joseph Müller, Berlin
78 x 55,5 x 62 cm
verchromtes Stahlrohr; Pergament-Polsterung /
chromium-plated tubular steel; vellum upholstery
Collection Vitra Design Museum, Weil am Rhein

127
André Waterkeyn
Architekturmodell 1:100 (Volumenmodell) /
architectural model 1:100 (volume model)
Atomium
1958
(Modell von ca. 1958, erneuert 2010 / model from c. 1958, renovated 2010)
137 x 140 x 140 cm
lackierter Zement; lackiertes Holz; lackiertes Metall; Beton / lacquered cement; lacquered wood; lacquered metal; concrete
Collection Vitra Design Museum, Weil am Rhein

Seit Joseph Paxtons Londoner *Kristallpalast* 1851 ist es üblich geworden, auf den Weltausstellungen die Auflösung von Materie, die Schönheit des Lichts und die Kontrolle über die Energie als Symbole des technischen Fortschritts in Form imposanter Bauwerke zu inszenieren.

Ever since Joseph Paxton's *Crystal Palace* of 1851 in London, it has become a common feature at World's Fairs and other international expositions to stage the dissolution of matter, the beauty of light, and the control of energy in imposing monuments that function as symbols of technological progress.

128
Ludwig Mies van der Rohe
Couchtisch / coffee table
MR 150/3
ca. 1929
Bamberg Metallwerkstätten, Berlin
48 x 99,7 x 99,7 cm
verchromter Stahl; Glas / chrome-plated steel; glass
Collection Sebastian Jacobi

Diese einzigartige Fassung des auch für die Brünner *Villa Tugendhat* realisierten Couchtisches wurde womöglich für den Messeauftritt der IG Farben auf der Weltausstellung 1929 in Barcelona entworfen. Subtil und gemächlich löst hier Mies van der Rohe Gewicht in Leichtigkeit und Statik in Bewegung auf.

This unique version of the coffee table also realized for the *Villa Tugendhat* in Brno was probably designed for the IG Farben presentation at the 1929 World's Fair in Barcelona. With subtle and leisurely ease, Mies van der Rohe dissolves weight into lightness and statics into movement.

TRANSPARENZ / TRANSPARENCY

129
David Colwell
Sessel / lounge chair
Contour Chair
1967/68
Trannon Furniture Ltd., Salisbury
61 x 77,7 x 71,5 cm
Acrylglas; Edelstahl / acrylic glass; high-grade steel
Collection Vitra Design Museum, Weil am Rhein

130
J. De Pas, D. D'Urbino, P. Lomazzi, C. Scolari
Armsessel / armchair
No. 270 (Blow)
1967
Zanotta spa, Nova Milanese, MI
83 x 110 x 97,5 cm
PVC
Collection Vitra Design Museum, Weil am Rhein

In diesem ersten aufblasbaren Wohnmöbel, das in großen Stückzahlen seriell produziert wurde, verwirklichte sich die Vision der Bauhäusler aus den 1920er Jahren, eines Tages auf einer „elastischen Luftsäule" sitzen zu können. Und indem er die Masse auflöste, hob der ebenso preiswerte, leichte und platzsparende wie kurzlebige Polstersessel die konventionellen Wohnvorstellungen gleich mit auf.

The first piece of inflatable furniture for the home to be serially produced in large quantities, this design realized the 1920s Bauhaus vision of one day being able to sit on an "elastic column of air". And by dispelling mass, this inexpensive, lightweight, and space-saving (and often short-lived) easy chair simultaneously did away with conventional notions of living.

131
Wilhelm Wagenfeld
Teeservice / tea service
1930–1934
Jenaer Glaswerke Schott & Gen., Jena
13 x 50 x 40 cm
farbloses feuerfestes Jenaer Glas /
transparent fire-proof Jena glass
Collection Alexander von Vegesack, Lessac-Confolens

Zwei Ideale des Bauhauses, Funktionalität und Klarheit, sind in diesem Service sinnvoll vereint.

Two ideals of the Bauhaus—functionality and clarity—are sensibly united in this tea service.

132

Naoto Fukasawa
Stuhl / chair
Chair (Acrylic)
2007
Vitra AG, Basel
80 x 47 x 59 cm
Acrylglas / acrylic glass
Collection Vitra Design Museum, Weil am Rhein

Seiner Serie *Chair* für die zweite Vitra Edition legte Naoto Fukasawa eine ideelle, allgemeingültige Grundform des Stuhls als geschlossenes Volumen zugrunde, die er in unterschiedlichen Materialien realisierte. Jede Variante interpretiert den Stuhl – und mithin das Sitzen – unter einem anderen Aspekt, stets werden jedoch unsere optische und haptische Wahrnehmung auf die Probe gestellt. In dieser Fassung verschwindet vielleicht der Gegenstand, hinterlässt aber umso klarer den Stuhl als Idee.

For his contribution to the second Vitra Edition programme, Naoto Fukasawa based his *Chair* series on an ideal, universal form—the chair as a closed volume—which he realized in various materials. Each variant interprets the chair—and thus the act of sitting—from a different angle, in each case putting our visual and haptic perception to the test. In this version, the material object almost seems to vanish, leaving behind the idea of the chair with all the more clarity.

133

Philippe Starck
Stuhl / chair
La Marie
1998
Kartell spa, Noviglio, MI
86,5 x 39 x 52,5 cm
Polykarbonat / polycarbonate
Collection Vitra Design Museum, Weil am Rhein

134

Joe & Gianni Colombo
Schreibtischlampe / desk lamp
No. 281 (Acrilica)
1962
Oluce spa, San Giuliano Milanese, MI
23,4 x 25,5 x 23,5 cm
Acrylharz; lackiertes Metall / acrylic resin; lacquered metal
Collection Vitra Design Museum, Weil am Rhein

Wie eine Teleportation aus den unergründlichen Tiefen des Raums demonstriert diese Leuchte das Licht als immateriellen, gerichteten Strahl.

Like a teleportation transmitted from the unfathomable depths of space, this lamp demonstrates light as an immaterial, targeted beam.

ZEICHEN / SIGN

135

Naoto Fukasawa
CD-Player
2004
Ryohin Keikaku Co. Ltd. (MUJI), Tokyo
17 x 17 x 4 cm
verschiedene Materialien / mixed media
Collection Mathias Schwartz-Clauss

Eine Quadratur des Kreises: Die dem Auge und der Hand schmeichelnden abgerundeten Ecken (die Kurven sind) versinnbildlichen die Einheit der unterschiedlichen Funktionen, was gerade im Falle technischer Geräte Vertrauen in die verborgenen Vorgänge schafft.

A squaring of the circle: pleasing the eye as well as the hand, the rounded corners (which are in fact curves) epitomize the unity of the various functions and, especially in the case of technical devices, instil trust in hidden processes.

136

Lautsprecher / loudspeaker
1926
Philips, Eindhoven
ca. 50 x 19 x 28 cm
Bakelit / bakelite
Collection Alexander von Vegesack, Lessac-Confolens

Ein Klangkörper in der Form zweier aufeinander folgender Schallwellen, hergestellt aus dem ersten, Anfang des 20. Jahrhunderts entwickelten industriellen Kunststoff.

A speaker in the form of two successive sound waves, manufactured from the first industrial plastic that was developed at the beginning of the twentieth century.

137

Eero Saarinen
Drehstuhl / swivel chair
No. 151 (Pedestal, Tulip)
1956
Knoll Associates, Inc., New York, NY
81,2 x 50 x 53,8 cm
glasfaserverstärktes Polyester, lackiert; lackierter Aluminiumguss; Schaumgummi; Stoff / glass-reinforced polyester, lacquered; lacquered cast aluminium; foam rubber; fabric
Collection Vitra Design Museum, Weil am Rhein

Charakteristisch für die *Tulip*-Möbelserie ist die auf einen Stiel reduzierte Stütze, wie bei einem Weinglas. Für Eero Saarinens ursprüngliche Idee, den ganzen Stuhl aus einem einzigen Kunststoffteil herzustellen, fehlten damals die technischen Möglichkeiten. Umso deutlicher hebt dieser Prototyp einer nie produzierten drehbaren Variante die formale Geschlossenheit des Entwurfs hervor.

Characteristic of the *Tulip* furniture series is the reduction of the base to a stem, as in a wine glass. Eero Saarinen originally sought to manufacture the entire chair from a single piece of plastic but the technical possibilities were lacking at the time. In this prototype for a never-produced swivel variant, the self-contained form of the design comes especially to the fore.

138

Bodo Rasch
Stuhl / chair
Zweischalenstuhl
1961
Bodo Rasch, Oberaichen
76,9 x 48 x 50,9 cm
gebogenes Sperrholz, lackiert; Stahl / bent plywood, lacquered; steel
Collection Vitra Design Museum, Weil am Rhein

139

Jacques Le Chevallier, René Koechlin
Tischlampe / table lamp
Chistera
1927–30
31 x 39 x 14,3 cm
Aluminiumblech; Bakelit / sheet aluminium; bakelite
Collection Vitra Design Museum, Weil am Rhein

140

Verner Panton
Stuhl / chair
Panton-Chair
1958–67
Vitra AG, Basel
81,5 x 51 x 61,5 cm
verchromtes Polypropylen / chromium-plated polypropylene
Collection Vitra Design Museum, Weil am Rhein

Diese 2005 einmalig versuchte verchromte Ausführung für eine Oberflächenprobe betont den ununterbrochenen Schwung einer Designikone, die das Sitzen als Geste zeigt.

This unique chrome-plated version, created as a surface sample, emphasizes the continuous curve of a chair that has become a design icon and that presents sitting as a gesture.

141

Eileen Gray
Beistelltisch / occasional table
(für das *Haus E-1027*) / (for the *E-1027 House*)
1925–28
Atelier Eileen Gray, Paris
58 x 41,1 x 41 cm
Stahlrohr; lackiertes Holz / tubular steel; lacquered wood
Collection Vitra Design Museum, Weil am Rhein

Form und Funktion werden hier zu einer nicht weiter zu reduzierenden Formel zusammengefasst, die das Anheben, Tragen und Abstellen des Beistelltisches auf den Punkt bringt.

Form and function are combined here to produce a formula beyond further reduction, getting straight to the point when it comes to the lifting, carrying, and setting down of this side table.

142

Mario Bellini
automatischer Plattenspieler / automatic record player
Phono Boy
1968
Grundig AG, Fürth
22,5 x 20 x 8,2 cm
Kunststoff; Metall / ABS plastic; metal
Collection Vitra Design Museum, Weil am Rhein

143

Shiro Kuramata
Stuhl / chair
Ko-Ko
1985
Idée, Tokyo
62,5 x 50 x 45 cm
lackiertes Holz; verchromtes Stahlrohr / lacquered wood; chrome-plated tubular steel
Collection Vitra Design Museum, Weil am Rhein

144

Alessandro Mendini
Stuhlobjekt / chair object
Lassù
1974
Alessandro Mendini, Milano
136 x 85 x 85 cm
gefärbtes Holz, halbverbrannt / stained wood, semi-burnt
Collection Vitra Design Museum, Weil am Rhein

In einem Happening vor den Büros der von ihm herausgegebenen Zeitschrift *Casabella* setzte Alessandro Mendini 1974 zwei identische, als *Lassù* (ital.: dort oben / dort hinauf) betitelte Stuhlobjekte in Flammen; dies hier ist eines davon. Mit seiner Verbrennung wurde der auf einer Pyramide thronende Stuhl als Sinnbild für den zeit- und gesichtslosen Archetyp infrage gestellt. Zugleich wurde ihm aber die Dimension der Zeit auch eingeschrieben. Übrig bleibt ein rätselhaftes Objekt, in dem sich Ewigkeit und Vergänglichkeit die Waage halten.

In a 1974 happening in front of the offices of *Casabella* magazine of which he was editor-in-chief, Alessandro Mendini set fire to two identical chair objects entitled *Lassù* (Italian for "up there") .Here is one of them. Enthroned on a pyramid and then burnt, the timeless and faceless archetype of the chair was thus symbolically called into question. At the same time, however, it was also inscribed with the dimension of time. What remains is an enigmatic object striking a balance between eternity and transience.

145

Gerrit T. Rietveld
Stuhl / chair
Zig zag
1932
G. T. Rietveld, Utrecht, für / for Metz & Co., Amsterdam
74 x 37 x 43 cm
lackiertes Holz; Metall / lacquered wood; metal
Collection Alexander von Vegesack, Lessac-Confolens

Nur mit aufwändigen Schwalbenschwanzverbindungen

sowie verleimten und verschraubten Stützleisten
gelingt Gerrit Rietveld die waghalsige Konstruktion einer
geknickten Fläche im Raum. Wie eine technische Propor-
tionsstudie zur Gestalt des sitzenden Körpers wirkt dieser
Entwurf, mit dem der Tischler und Architekt auf den
funktionalistischen Minimalismus seiner Zeit antwortet.

It took elaborate dovetail joints as well as glued and
bolted support strips for Gerrit Rietveld to achieve this
daring construction of a bent plane in space. As the
cabinetmaker and architect's response to the functional-
istic minimalism of the time, this design comes across
as a technical proportional study of the human figure in
sitting position.

146
Ettore Sottsass Jr.
Kommode / cabinet
Cubirolo
1966/67
Poltronova srl, Agliana, PT
67,6 x 45,2 x 49,8 cm
gefärbtes Holz; Formica / ebonized wood; Formica
Collection Vitra Design Museum, Weil am Rhein

Wie kleine Zielscheiben oder, besser noch, bunte Knöpfe
machen die Knäufe auf sich aufmerksam und signalisieren:
Öffne mich!

Like miniature bull's eye targets or, even better, colourful
buttons, the knobs draw attention to themselves and call
out: Open me!

147
Pietro Chiesa
Stehlampe / floor lamp
Luminator
1933
FontanaArte spa, Corsico, MI
190 x 33 x 31,5 cm
Messing; Metallblech / brass; sheet metal
Collection Vitra Design Museum, Weil am Rhein

Mit seiner stoischen Ausrichtung und dem goldenen
Glanz erinnert der Deckenstrahler an eine gen Himmel
gerichtete Fanfare oder den Kegel eines Flakscheinwer-
fers, wie ihn Albert Speer drei Jahre später in seinen
Lichtdomen für nationalsozialistische Propaganda nutzte.

With its stoic stance and golden sheen, this floor lamp
evokes the image of a fanfare directed to the heavens
or the cone of a search light, as used by Albert Speer three
years later in the light domes he created for National
Socialist propaganda.

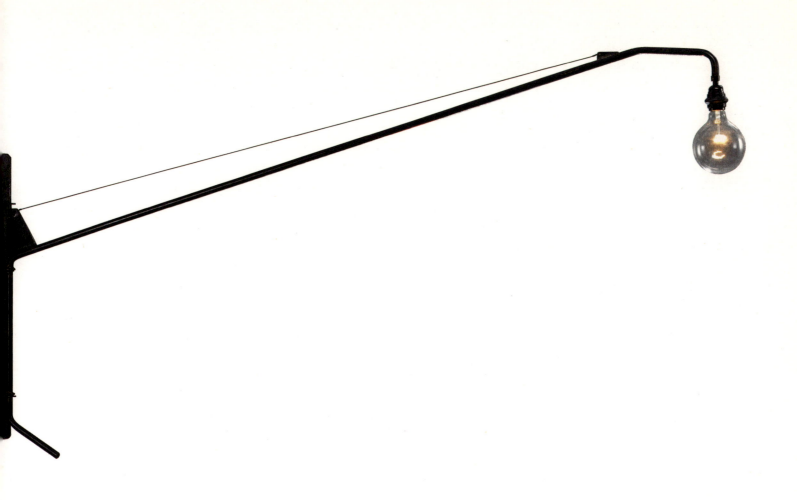

JEAN PROUVÉ
Potence
1950
Collection Vitra Design Museum,
Weil am Rhein

Martin Hartung

DER MENSCH ALS MAß ALLER DINGE? /
MAN AS THE MEASURE OF ALL THINGS?

Das ist das Design, das aller
Kultur zugrunde liegt: die Natur
dank Technik überlisten, Natür-
liches durch Künstliches über-
treffen und Maschinen bauen,
aus denen ein Gott fällt, der wir
selbst sind.

This is the design that is the
basis of all culture: to deceive
nature by means of technology,
to replace what is natural
with what is artificial and build
a machine out of which there
comes a god who is ourselves.

Vilém Flusser

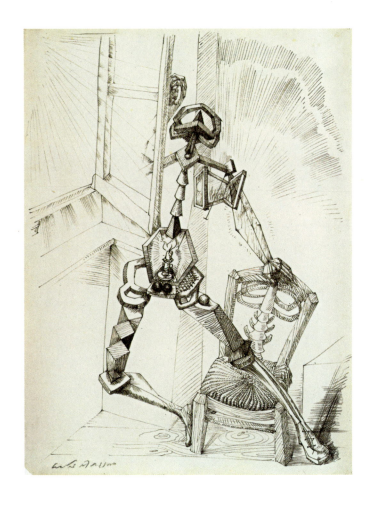

André Masson, Naissance de l'automate
(Die Geburt des Automaten), 1938, Tusche,
63 x 48 cm, Sammlung Scharf-Gerstenberg,
Staatliche Museen zu Berlin.

André Masson, Naissance de l'automate
(The Birth of the Automat), ink drawing,
63 x 48 cm, Collection Scharf-Gerstenberg,
Staatliche Museen zu Berlin.

In seinen Erörterungen zu Protagoras' Ausspruch „Der Mensch ist das Maß aller Dinge" zitierte der Philosoph Clemens Sedmak kürzlich eine Passage aus den Erinnerungen des Holocaust-Überlebenden Primo Levi, der sich die Brotausgabe in Auschwitz ins Gedächtnis rief: „[...] in fünf Minuten wird Brot ausgegeben [...] dieser heilige, graue Würfel, der dir in der Hand deines Nächsten so riesig vorkommt und in deiner eigenen so klein, dass du weinen könntest."[1] Der Frage nach einem menschlichen Maß in den Dingen wird also mit Bedacht zu begegnen sein. Denn macht man sich daran, das Wesen der Dinge zu ergründen, kommt man nicht umhin, die Frage nach dem Wesen des Menschen zu stellen. Der Mensch ist das Wesen, das Dinge hat. Oder: Die Welt des Menschen besteht aus Dingen.

Mit der Entdeckung der Röntgenstrahlen im Jahr 1895 durfte man wahrhaft glauben, das Wesen der Dinge ergründet zu haben. Die Objekte ließen sich fortan enthüllen und eine „andere Natur der Dinge" offenbarte sich. In den Fabriken ahmten Automaten die Gesten des Menschen nach, während die Arbeiter am Fließband ihre Produkte sich im Raum bewegen sahen und selbst gezwungen waren still zu stehen. Mithin entstand das Bedürfnis nach einer Ästhetik und Kultur, die den Menschen als einen von seinen Dingen Entfremdeten wieder mit der Welt versöhnen sollte. Zur

Der Mensch als Industriepalast, didaktisches Poster aus Fritz Kahn: „Das Leben des Menschen" (Stuttgart, 1926–31), 95,7 x 48 cm, Westfälisches Schulmuseum.

Poyet, Récréations photographiques (Röntgenstrahlen), Illustration in: La Nature, 1897, Bd. 2, S. 32, 19 x 28 cm.

Der Mensch als Industriepalast (Man as Industrial Palace), didactic poster accompanying Fritz Kahn's "Das Leben des Menschen" (Stuttgart, 1926–31), 95,7 x 48 cm, Westfälisches Schulmuseum.

Poyet, Récréations photographiques (X-rays), Illustration in: La Nature, 1897, vol. 2, p. 32, 19 x 28 cm.

Veranschaulichung der Prozesse, die die Gesellschaft mechanisierten, bot sich das Nächstliegende an: der menschliche Körper. Nachdem die Moderne diesen einer zunehmenden Disziplinierung unterworfen hatte, konnte die Maschine sogar zum Sinnbild des Körpers stilisiert werden. Die Plakatbeilage zu einer Publikation des deutschen Frauenarztes und Schriftstellers Fritz Kahn aus dem Jahr 1926 stellt den menschlichen Körper in Maschinenmetaphern dar, wobei eine Analogie zwischen den organischen Verdauungsmechanismen und der Organisation einer Chemiefabrik hergestellt wird. Der Mensch ist hier nicht das Maß, vielmehr wird er gemessen – an der Automation, die schon dem Wortlaut nach das Potenzial hat, auch ohne seine Gegenwart zu funktionieren.

Anders als Kahn thematisierte der Bauhauslehrer Oskar Schlemmer zwei Jahre später in einer Studienzeichnung den ganzen Menschen als einen Akteur im Zentrum, der aus dem Raum seiner Ideen heraus die ihn umgebende Welt (wieder) prägen kann. Im linken Bildteil der Zeichnung findet sich eine 1916 entwickelte Grundfigur des Künstlers, die auf eine als allgemeingültig angelegte Typengestaltung verweist, wie sie wenig später die Bestrebungen des Bauhaus kennzeichnete. Neben einer „Reduktion aller gegenständlichen Erscheinungen auf geometrische Grundformen" erklärte

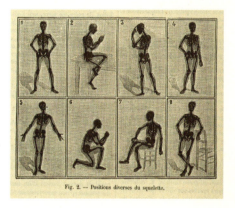

book published in 1926 by German gynaecologist and author Fritz Kahn depicts the human body in machine metaphors, creating an analogy between the organic mechanisms of digestion and the organization of a chemical factory. Here man is not the measure but is being measured—measured against an automaton that, as the word indicates, has the potential to function without human presence.

In contrast to Kahn, the Bauhaus teacher Oskar Schlemmer created a sketch two years later that positioned the individual as a central protagonist able to (once again) shape the world around him based on the realm of his ideas. The left part of the drawing contains a basic character, developed by the artist in 1916, that refers to a universal design type, as would soon characterize the aims of the Bauhaus. Meanwhile, along with a "reduction of all representational phenomena to basic

In his deliberations on Protagoras' claim that "man is the measure of all things", the philosopher Clemens Sedmak cites a passage from the memoirs of Holocaust survivor Primo Levi that recalls the handing out of bread in Auschwitz: "[I]n five minutes begins the distribution of bread..., of the holy, grey slab which seems gigantic in your neighbour's hand, and in your own hand so small as to make you cry."[1] The question of human scale in material things is thus to be approached with caution, for when seeking to grasp the nature of things, it is impossible to avoid questioning the nature of man. Man is the being that has things. Or, in other words, the world of man consists of things.

With the discovery of X-rays in 1895, it must have seemed as though the nature of things had truly been fathomed. Objects could henceforth be exposed to reveal a "different nature of things" underneath. In factories, automated

machines imitated human gestures and workers on the assembly line saw their products moving along in space while they themselves were forced to remain stationary. Thus arose the need for an aesthetics and culture that would allow society to overcome its alienation from material things and reconcile it with the world. For the purpose of illustrating the processes that had mechanized society, the most obvious model to present itself was the human body. Having been increasingly disciplined in the modern era, the body could even be symbolized by the machine in stylized form. For example, the poster accompanying a

Walter Gropius in den Grundsätzen zur Bauhausproduktion die Erforschung des die Dinge bestimmenden Wesens zum Programm.[2] Als komprimiertes Konzept eines Funktionalismus, der sich zu diesem Zeitpunkt noch primär an Gegenständen orientierte, verwies Gropius' Diktum bereits auf den angestrebten Einsatz typisierter Bauformen.

Le Corbusier proklamierte schließlich in seinem 1922 verfassten Text *Vers une Architecture* das Haus als eine Maschine zum Wohnen, in der sich die modernen Errungenschaften mit den Denkmälern der Geschichte derart verschwistern, dass sogar der griechische Architekt „Phidias […] gern in dieser Zeit der Standardisierung gelebt" hätte.[3]

Im selben Jahr, in dem Gropius die Zweckvollendung der Dinge zum Anliegen des Baus erklärte, schilderte Le Corbusier seinen „l'homme type", den typischen Menschen, ausgestattet mit „meubles-types", deren einfache Form strikt funktional bestimmt sein sollte: Es galt, „den menschlichen Maßstab, die menschliche Funktion zu finden".[4] Die Befürworter einer reinen Funktionalität in Architektur und Design, die in ihren Idealvorstellungen immer auch die Handlungen des modernen Menschen mit entwerfen, mussten im Verlauf des 20. Jahrhunderts einsehen, dass in einem relationalen Gefüge

von Mensch und Ding gerade der Mensch in seinen Taten wie in seinen Einstellungen nur schwer zu kalkulieren ist.

Zu Beginn der 1930er Jahre machte sich der amerikanische Produktdesigner Henry Dreyfuss daran, mithilfe anthropometrischer und ergonomischer Daten die Bedürfnisse der Menschen in ein komplexes, interaktives Koordinatensystem einzuordnen, aus dem eine Vielzahl an Diagrammen hervorging, die als Maßstäbe zahlreicher Produktformen dienen sollten.[5] Diese Einbeziehung menschlicher Faktoren in das Design unternahm Dreyfuss beinahe ein Jahrzehnt vor der Formulierung des *Modulor*, den Le Corbusier seit 1943 gedanklich entwickelte und dessen Entwurf sich an Proportionsstudien der Antike orientierte.[6]

In der mathematischen Exaktheit und der Anwendung naturgegebener Proportionen folgt der *Modulor* Le Corbusiers dessen vorrangigem Bemühen um die Einführung eines universalen, funktionalen Maßes als Modul für eine standardisierte Massenproduktion nach dem Goldenen Schnitt. Mit dieser Maßgabe beabsichtigte Le Corbusier das Meter zu überwinden, das er als eine abstrakte, die Architektur gar „verrenkende" Maßeinheit betrachtete.[7]

„Selbst wußte ich nicht, wie es kam, daß ich einen unaussprechlichen Haß auf die warf, denen ich Schmuck gefertigt. […] Die Arbeit

Oskar Schlemmer, *Der Mensch im Ideenkreis*, 1928 (Detail). Unterrichtstafel für den Bühnenkurs „Der Mensch", Bauhaus Dessau. Feder und gesprühte Tusche, roter Farbstift und Deckweiss auf Papier, auf Karton aufgezogen, 51,5 x 38 cm. Bühnen Archiv Oskar Schlemmer, Sammlung UJS, Courtesy C. Raman Schlemmer.

Oskar Schlemmer, *Der Mensch im Ideenkreis* (Man in a Sphere of Ideas), 1928 (detail). Educational panel for the Bühnenkurs (stage course) "Der Mensch" (The Man) at Bauhaus Dessau. India ink, pencil, coloured pencil, and opaque white on paper, mounted on board, 51,5 x 38 cm. The Oskar Schlemmer Theatre Estate, Collection UJS, Courtesy C. Raman Schlemmer.

geometric forms", Walter Gropius declared research into the nature of objects as one of the principles of Bauhaus production.[2] As a condensed concept of the functionalism that was still primarily oriented to objects at the time, Gropius' dictum points ahead to the desire to make use of standardized building types. As for Le Corbusier, in his *Vers une Architecture* of 1922 he proclaimed the house as a machine for living, pairing modern achievements with monuments of history so that even the Greek architect "Pheidias would have loved to live in this era of standards".[3]

In the same year that Gropius declared the fulfilment of an object's function as a concern of design, Le Corbusier portrayed his "l'homme type", the typical man, as outfitted with "meubles-types" whose simple form was to be determined strictly according to function. The guiding aim was "to find the human scale, the human function".[4] Over the course of the twentieth century, the advocates of pure functionality in architecture and design, whose ideal conceptions had always been based on the actions of modern man, were forced to see that in the relational fabric between man and object, it was man who proved difficult to estimate in his actions and preferences.

In the early 1930s, the American product designer Henry Dreyfuss employed anthropometric and ergonomic data to classify human needs in a complex, interactive coordinate system that provided the basis for a multitude of diagrams, which were meant to serve as standards for numerous product forms.[5] This incorporation of human factors in design was undertaken by Dreyfuss nearly a decade before the formulation of the *Modulor*, which Le Corbusier had been conceptually developing since 1943 and whose scheme is based on Antiquity's study of proportions.[6]

In its mathematical precision and its utilization of proportions found in nature, Le Corbusier's *Modulor* pursues the primary aim of introducing a universal and functional measurement as a module for standardized mass production based on the Golden Ratio. With this stipulation, Le Corbusier sought to supplant the meter, which he regarded as an abstract unit of measurement that "dislocates" architecture.[7]

"I myself do not know how it happened, but I developed an inexpressible hatred for those for whom

Le Corbusier, „Besoins types, meubles types“,
Illustration zu dessen Artikel „Exposition des Arts
Decoratifs“, in: *L'Esprit Nouveau* 23, Mai 1924, o.S.

Le Corbusier, "Besoins types, meubles types",
illustration for his article "Exposition des Arts
Decoratifs", in: *L'Esprit Nouveau* 23, May 1924.

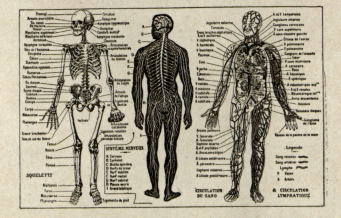

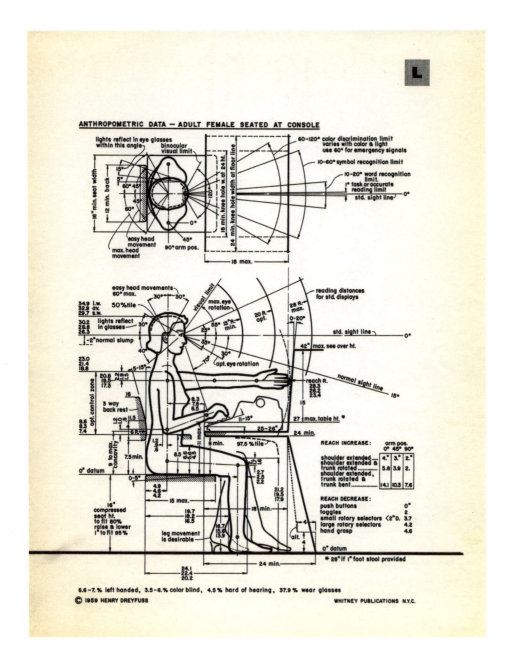

Anthropometric Data – Adult Female Seated at
Console (Anthropometrische Daten einer erwachsenen
Frau am Steuerpult sitzend), Blatt „L" aus:
Henry Dreyfuss' „The Measure of Man. Human Factors in
Design" (New York, 1959).

Anthropometric Data—Adult Female Seated at
Console, sheet "L" in: Henry Dreyfuss' "The Measure
of Man. Human Factors in Design" (New York,
Whitney Library of Design, 1959).

gelang mir wie keine andere, aber es zerriss mir die Brust, wenn ich daran dachte, mich von dem Schmuck, der mein Herzenskleinod geworden, trennen zu müssen", lässt E.T.A. Hoffmann den Goldschmied Cardillac sagen, der nicht ertragen kann, dass sich das Werk seiner Hände regelmäßig in eine Ware verwandelt – weshalb er die Käufer schließlich mit dem Leben bezahlen lässt, um seine Schöpfungen zurückzugewinnen.[8] Was auf Cardillac noch wie ein Fluch lastet, wird schon bald zur massenhaften Wirklichkeit. Mit der im 19. Jahrhundert zunehmenden Spezialisierung und Segmentierung der Arbeit folgte die Entfremdung des Menschen von seinen Dingen. Die Maschine „braucht nicht mehr die Hand, sondern nur noch Hände".[9] Das Geschenk des Prometheus machte den Menschen zum *homo faber*, dessen größte Verantwortung entzündete sich jedoch erst an den Feuern der Industrie.

1 Primo Levi: *Ist das ein Mensch? Erinnerungen an Auschwitz*, Frankfurt a. M. 1979, S. 39, zit. nach: Clemens Sedmak: „Menschlichkeit. Überlegungen zu einem Maß des Ethischen", in: Otto Neumair (Hrsg.): *Ist der Mensch das Maß aller Dinge?*, Reihe Arianna. Wunschbilder der Antike, hrsg. v. Siegrid Düll und Otto Neumaier, Bd. 4. Möhnesee 2004, S. 229–252, hier S. 230.

2 „Auch der Mensch ist nur aus krummem Holz", in: *Der Spiegel*, Nr. 47, 1979, S. 232–241, hier S. 234.

3 Le Corbusier: *Ausblick auf eine Architektur*, Frankfurt a. M., Berlin 1963, S. 114.

4 Stanislaus von Moos: „Ronèo Büromöbel", in: *L'Esprit Nouveau. Le Corbusier und die Industrie 1920–1925*, Ausst.-Kat. Museum für Gestaltung Zürich et al., hrsg. v. ders., Zürich 1987, S. 275.

5 Vgl. Henry Dreyfuss: *The Measure of Man. Human Factors in Design*. Two Life Size Figure Charts Suitable for Mounting, (Beilage), New York 1960.

6 Vgl. Le Corbusier: *Modulor 2*, 4. Aufl. Stuttgart 1990 [1955]. Sowie u.a. Frank Zöllner: „Anthropomorphismus in der Architektur. Das Maß des Menschen in der Architektur von Vitruv bis Le Corbusier", in: Neumair (Hrsg.), a.a.O., S. 307–343 (vgl. Anm. 1).

7 Le Corbusier: *Modulor 2*, a.a.O., S. 20.

8 E.T.A. Hoffmann: „Das Fräulein von Scuderie", in: *Die Serapionsbrüder II*, Berlin 1985, S. 225f. und S. 228.

9 Lu Märten: *Wesen und Veränderung der Formen und Künste*, Weimar 1949, S. 205.

I made jewellery. … The work succeeded like none other, but it tore me apart when I thought of having to part with those jewels, which had become my heart's treasure." So says E. T. A. Hoffman's Cardillac, the goldsmith who, in "Mademoiselle de Scudery", cannot bear the fact that the work of his hands regularly ends up transformed into a commodity and who ultimately makes buyers pay with their lives in order to recover his creations.[8] What weighs on Cardillac like a curse soon establishes itself as wide-scale reality. With the increasing specialization and segmentation of work in the nineteenth century, society became increasingly alienated from material things. The machine "no longer has need for the hand but only for more hands".[9] The gift of Prometheus turned man into *Homo faber*, yet his greatest responsibility was sparked much later in the fires of industry.

1 Primo Levi, *If this is a Man*, trans. Stuart Woolf (London: Orion Press, 1959), 36. German translation quoted in Clemens Sedmak, "Menschlichkeit: Überlegungen zu einem Maß des Ethischen", in *Ist der Mensch das Maß aller Dinge?*, ed. Otto Neumair (Möhnesee: Bibliopolis, 2004), 229–252.

2 "Auch der Mensch ist nur aus krummem Holz", *Der Spiegel* 47 (1979), 234.

3 Le Corbusier, *Toward an Architecture*, trans. John Goodman (Los Angeles: Getty Publications, 2007), 189.

4 Stanislaus von Moos, "Ronéo Büromöbel", in *L'Esprit Nouveau: Le Corbusier und die Industrie, 1920–1925*, exhibition catalogue, ed. idem (Zurich: Museum für Gestaltung Zürich, 1987), 275.

5 See Henry Dreyfuss, *The Measure of Man: Human Factors in Design*, incl. two life-size figure charts suitable for mounting (New York: Whitney Library of Design, 1960).

6 See Le Corbusier, *Modulor*, 2 vols., 4th ed. (Stuttgart: Deutsche Verlags-Anstalt, 1990 [1948]). See also Frank Zöllner, "Anthropomorphismus in der Architektur: Das Maß des Menschen in der Architektur von Vitruv bis Le Corbusier", in *Ist der Mensch das Maß aller Dinge?*, ed. Otto Neumair (Möhnesee: Bibliopolis, 2004), 307–343.

7 Le Corbusier, *Modulor*, 20.

8 E. T. A. Hoffmann, "Mademoiselle de Scudery", in *Tales of Hoffmann*, trans. R. J. Hollingdale (London: Penguin, 1982), 65, 68.

9 Lu Märten, *Wesen und Veränderung der Formen und Künste* (Weimar: Werden und Wirken, 1949), 205.

VORBILD /
MODEL

148

149

150

151

153

152

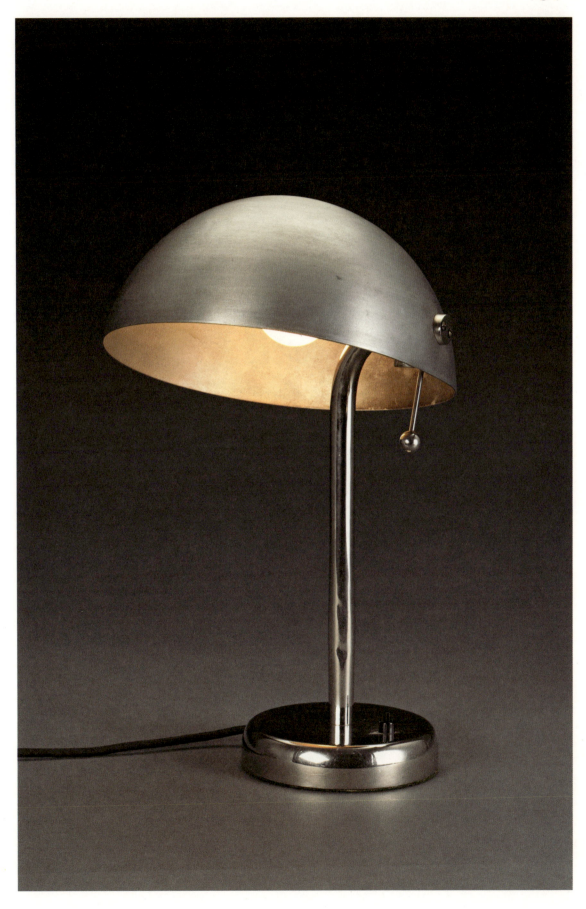

155

156

157

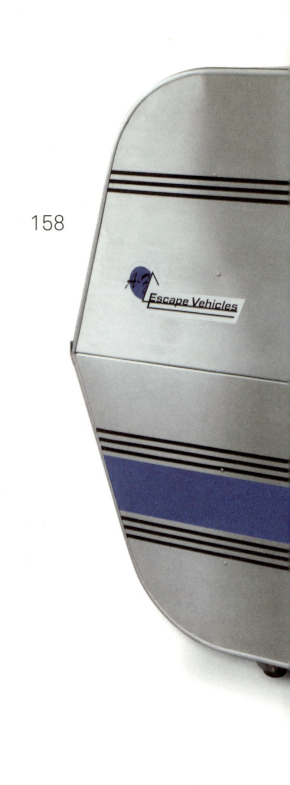

158